Just A Vessel

Gregory R Reid

JUST A VESSEL

ISBN: 9798694210416

DEDICATION

For Rob and Jennifer, who loved Stray Cats and wanted more. Here you are, my loved friends.

JUST A VESSEL

FOREWORD

One of my first books was called *Stray Cats*. It was a very vulnerable, honest, sometimes funny, but always heartfelt collection of stories from my life and ministry. They were stories about people, family, real ministry, and its cost as I saw demonstrated by the faithful Jesus servants I was blessed to know.

Many years later, I have written another book almost as a bookend to *Stray Cats* without knowing it. Originally titled "Stones of Remembrance," I had compiled several significant memories where Jesus totally invaded my life and changed me from the inside out. There are stories of real-life lessons taught by the Holy Spirit in His gentle, determined way.

Theological and topical books are important. But when it comes down to it, Jesus died for sinners so we could have a *relationship* with Him - and with each other.

So here are more stories – vulnerable, heartfelt and real stories about how Jesus touched and changed my life. It's also about how He used this vessel – this clay pot – and filled it with His love and glory and allowed me to touch others as well.

The photo on the front is an example of the Japanese art of Kintsugi – repairing, rather than discarding, broken pottery. It's so like our Father, who "rebuilds Jerusalem on her ruins." The idea behind Kintsugi is that it treats breakage and repair as part of the history of an object, rather than something to disguise.

"We hold this treasure in earthen vessels," Paul said. And though he sometimes breaks and remakes us on His potter's wheel, it is only to repair and use us in a greater way. I pray in each of these stories you will discover, in your weaknesses and fears, your worth and your value to the Father who called you His "poema" – His workmanship – His poem - a beautiful poem He is writing with His own heart and hand in the precious moments in your life where you and He meet, and He changes you forever.

Gregory R Reid

October 20th 2020

1 ANGEL IN AN LTD

There was a big old boat of a car in the 1960s-1970s called an LTD. I don't think there's anything like it today.

Before I got saved, I hitchhiked a lot. I don't recommend it at all. As a fourteen-year-old boy, it was stupid and dangerous, but I needed a ride…

Several times I got picked up by preachers. They always had little VW Beetles with stuck passenger doors that couldn't open up except from the outside. Which meant you got out when the preacher got through preaching to you.

I was desperately lost and in darkness, seeking truth, practicing the occult, ensnared in a demonic work with no way out.

A lady handed me a tiny New Testament in a department store called Zody's. She said she would pray for me. I kept it, but I didn't read it. Preacher One in a Volkswagen told me about Jesus. I know, I said.

Preacher Two in a VW told me Jesus loved me. What was it with these guys, I wondered? Same car, same speech. "I know," I told him. "No, I don't think you understand," he said, turning to look me straight in the eyes. "God woke me up this morning and told me to drive out here. I live in Manhattan Beach. That's 45 miles away! God told me there would be a young boy hitchhiking on the corner of Topanga and Valley Circle, and I was to pick him up and tell him Jesus loves him. And you're that boy!"

Now I was scared. My first thought was that the guy was crazy. My second thought was, how did he know? I studied psychics. I tried to *be* one! But *nobody* got this accurate. My third thought was…what if? What if God *did* send him? But no, because my fourth thought was, "It can't be. God can't love me. I'm evil." Devastated by abuse and darkness growing up, I'd come to believe that I was evil, and if there was a God, He could never love me after everything I'd done.

But here this guy was: "Jesus loves you." "I know," I said. (I lied. I didn't know that at all. But what *if*?)

He prayed with me, and I walked away all achy and longing and lost.

A few months later, my closest friend – a die-hard, argue-you-into-the-ground atheist and I were hitchhiking to see his girlfriend.

An LTD pulled over…

I'm safe, I thought. It's not a VW. No preacher driver.

It was worse, for inside was a mid-50's, on fire for God "Jesus Freak." (That's what we called them then – not knowing what I know now, that Jesus doesn't turn people into freaks. He turns freaks into people.) From the moment we got in, he started telling us about this "cool" house meeting where people got together and talked about God…

Did not want to go. Was sure my atheist friend was about to go off on him…

2

…Instead, he listened, politely. Ted — that was his name — gave my friend a card with the address of the house they were meeting at that night.

My friend said nothing. We went to his girlfriend's house. She wasn't home. "Let's go to this deal," my friend said as he took the card out of his shirt pocket. It turned out that the house meeting was just a few blocks away. I was totally shocked. "Okayyy," I said suspiciously. I'd never seen my friend so quiet.

We got to the house. The front door was open. The house was packed, wall-to-wall people — kids, couples, old people and little kids, teens like us. We found seating across the living room from each other.

The house owner and leader, Dave Malkin, was telling everyone how Jesus loved them and how to become a Christian. I froze. It was just a few weeks after the VW guy from Manhattan beach picked me up and told me that.

I blocked out a lot of that night. But I remember Dave having everyone close their eyes as he explained how to get "saved." He explained what it was to give your life to Jesus. When he asked for anyone who wanted to pray to receive Jesus to raise their hand, I had to peek.

My friend's hand went up. It was the very last thing I ever expected to see. Dave led everyone in the "sinner's prayer."

The meeting ended, and I saw Dave talking to my friend for a while.

Ted- Mr. LTD – took us home. My friend sat in the front seat, and he and Ted talked about Jesus the whole time like they had known each other for years. I felt alone...scared...I was losing my best friend, my last friend, to Jesus, but I still couldn't believe that Jesus could love *me*.

Ted gave both of us a *Good News for Modern Man* Bible and copies of "The Cross and the Switchblade" by David Wilkerson.

My friend made me swear I'd go back with him. We'd been friends since we were ten. His life had been so cruel and sad. I promised I'd go back. His mom beat him when he got home and said he could never go back to that "Jesus freak" meeting again. He never did.

I was sooo lost. I was so buried in demonic darkness with no way out.

A few weeks (or months?) later, I was hitchhiking again...alone. A big LTD pulled over. The door opened. "Hi, Greg!" Ted said as I got in. "H...how do you remember my name?" I stammered. "Well, I haven't stopped praying for you since I saw you at Action Life. Hey, can I take you to dinner?" "I'll have to call my parents," I said, and I did, hoping Mom would say no. (She would, right? This was a stranger...I was 14... say *no*, Mom!) "Sure, honey. Just be back by nine." Now I was trapped!

"How are things with you and Jesus?" Ted asked as I poked at a steak at Love's Barbecue Pit. "Fine," which was a lie. Which I'm sure he knew. I wasn't even what they would call "saved." "Don't give up, Greg," Ted said. "Jesus loves you so much." I nodded, inwardly screaming "No, He doesn't! He *can't!* I'm evil!"

He dropped me off home after inviting me to Action Life again.

My desperation was pushing me to not wanting to live anymore. Every muscle and bone in my body ached from loneliness, rejection, feeling like dirt.

I went on a business trip with my parents. I brought The Cross and the Switchblade. I read it. When I read how this skinny preacher David Wilkerson faced down – and got beaten by – Nicky Cruz, a killer gang leader, and told him, "You can cut me up in a thousand pieces, Nicky and every piece is going to scream out, "Jesus loves you!", those three words plunged into my heart deep and painful. They made me angry, sad, and feeling even more lost. I was so angry. I threw the book into the wall across the room. "Why didn't *anyone* ever tell me God could love the worst person? That God had this kind of *power?*" (Only later did I realize…He had…and Ted was the last of many.)

We went home the next day. That night after settling in and closing myself away in my room, I lay down and cried out to whatever God or being was there if there was any. I asked someone, anyone, to save me, to help me, because I didn't want to live in that kind of pain anymore and wasn't going to anymore.

The full story of what happened next was written in my biography, *Nobody's Angel.* I was literally taken to heaven and held in the arms of Jesus, feeling loved for the first time in my life. It was the most real moment of my whole life, and I was returned to my bed crying, and knowing Jesus was real.

The next day, I began to talk to Jesus, though I didn't yet really know Him. And one night a month or so later, I felt absolutely compelled to pull Ted's card out of my wallet and call him.

"Hey, Greg!" he said. "I've been waiting for you to call!" Now I was totally freaked out. "What do you mean?" I asked, very tense. "Oh, I put a poster up by your house about Action Life, and I asked Jesus to have you call me. And here you are! So you're coming tonight?" "Nope," I said a bit too firmly. "I've got plans. Maybe another time." "Oh, OK," Ted said, obviously disappointed. "Well, I'm praying for you!"

I hung up the phone, turned to my drinking buddies and said, "We're going to a Bible Study tonight." And we did! And on that night, my life changed forever, as I surrendered my heart to Jesus and was born again into eternal life, my sins forgiven, my heart made new!

Ted was *so* happy!

I saw Ted less frequently after that as my fifteen-year-old born-again soul met other kids, found a church, went to Action Life less, and felt an increasing pull to ministry, which led to Bible School and then full-time service in the Kingdom of God.

I never forgot Ted, but like with so many people in our lives, time and tide wash away memories, and they often take a quiet eddy in our hearts and minds. Not gone, just not often recalled.

One day, nearly nineteen years after I met Jesus, I was giving my testimony to a ragtag bunch of kids that I co-youth pastored – street kids, kids in deep trouble, kids without Jesus, kids few even wanted to tell about Jesus. I realized, suddenly, they were part of Ted's legacy. I realized I needed to let him know.

For like many of the unsung heroes of the faith, Ted just did what he did and probably never really knew if he really made much of a difference at all.

Was he even still alive?

I took a chance and made some calls to some people at Action Life I hadn't seen or talked to in years.

I got a number, I called, not knowing if Ted would even remember me. He did! I was West Coast bound that Christmas, so we arranged to meet.

I don't remember exactly where we met, except that it was right north of Roscoe and Owensmouth in Reseda. But I knew him right away when I saw him. He was probably late 60's or early 70's, but the Jesus sparkle in his eyes made the years disappear, and I saw the same joy that made me know this Jesus thing was different so many years before.

We spent a long time catching up on each other's lives, me in "professional" ministry, Ted just leading people to Jesus, year after year.

I told him about our youth ministry – to the hopeless, the unloved…kids like I had been…Finally, I took out a stack of photos from our youth group. "Take a look at your grandkids," I said, placing them in front of him.

He looked carefully at them, one by one, then, he couldn't contain his emotions. "Oh, hot, dog, hot dog!" he said, breaking out in tears with that old expression of unrestrained joy. "Ted," I said, fighting back my own tears, "They're with Jesus because you cared about me and cared enough to tell me about Jesus. When I met you, I didn't think anyone cared about me. When you picked me up that second time in your LTD and said, 'Hey Greg!' when I got in, it blew my mind. You REMEMBERED me. It was a miracle to me."

"Oh, you don't know what the real miracle is," Ted laughed and wiped away tears. "I remembered you, but I couldn't remember your name. I've *never* been good at names. But I prayed really quick as I pulled over to pick you up and said, 'Jesus tell me what his name is.' And Jesus immediately said, 'His name is Greg." That's the miracle!" Now it was my turn to let the tears fall. JESUS KNEW MY NAME! And he loved me enough to tell this gentle man of God that name so that fragile hurting kid would know that he *mattered*.

When I read now that "I called you by name" in the Bible, I know it to be true. How great, how loving, how powerful, how merciful is our savior!

And how gracious that He allowed me to track down this angel in an LTD and tell him that his life had reaped an eternal reward in the lives of kids he never even knew he touched!

I am fairly certain Ted has moved on by now, no doubt standing in God's presence and laughing, "Hot dog!" or just casting his reward crown at His feet.

Thank You, God, for sending an angel in an LTD, and letting me find him to tell him how much his life mattered to God, to me, to countless others.

God may have once sent you a human angel, as well. Maybe it's time you let them know!

JUST A VESSEL

2 KEEPING SCORE

For two years, I signed up as a counselor for middle school kids in New Mexico, something I wrote about more extensively in my story, "The Lame Prince." It was always a wonderful, challenging, strenuous, and rewarding week for me. They kept the kids (and their counselors!) running and playing from dawn till lights out. I suspect that youth pastors looking for the next job will probably find their motivation to put in applications that week, as they realize they can't keep up with the pace or the scores the younger kids have. Well, maybe in their early 20's, but those who endure and are still in the game in their 30's, 40's and even 50's are the real warriors of youth ministry. They're in it for the heart, not the score.

Evening services at this camp were always moments of real transformation and a touch from God. I wouldn't trade those weeks for anything. I came home from every camp beaten up, worn out, and charged up after seeing God at work in kids' lives for five days.

Camp games are rough and tumble, from relays to kickball to water balloon fights. Some I did, others I opted out of to protect my not-so-sturdy bones from undue breakage. But whether in the game or on the sidelines cheering, I always wanted to be in the middle of it all.

The scriptures speak many times of our journey on earth in terms of athletics: A race, a wrestling match, an Olympics game. When one gets beyond just being concerned with whether the Cowboys win this year or not, there are a lot of great parallels you can draw from sports for our spiritual walk: You have to play fair (God's heart) You have to play by the rules. (God's Word.) You have to know your opponents' weaknesses (spiritual warfare.)

Some sports figures can be brilliant theologians, like Vince Lombardi: "Fatigue makes a coward of us all." (See Elijah running from Jezebel for more clarity on that thought.)

For us as believers, winning isn't the point. It's the heart of the game.

I've seen dads in wheelchairs at their kid's games, dads who will never run for home base, who are screaming and as excited as if they were the one who could win or lose the game! They are just as much a part of the game as their child.

It is too easy to look at people "doing things for God" – people in ministry or the mission field – and think, "They are really important to the Kingdom of God. All I do is work and pray and send support to those who are important."

You couldn't be more wrong, friend. Not all of us can – or are called – to what we call "full-time ministry." Yet, Paul, in all his writings to the churches, always spoke of missions givers as his full partners – with a full reward with him!

God established this principle long ago through King David. They had gone to war, and one of the tribes had stayed behind looking after their stuff. Everyone got upset, but David decreed that the reward would be shared

– the same for the battle warriors as those who stayed with the stuff. (1 Samuel 30:24)

Your mission field may not be in Africa. It may be to raise godly kids. I recently had this conversation with a dear friend that somehow felt his life had not really amounted to much for Jesus. "Have you seen your kids?" I asked him. "Your daughter loves Jesus and is married to a worship leader. Your son loves Jesus and is a brilliant musician. That didn't happen by accident." I know many saints who had been taken out of great darkness into Jesus, and though their own lives suffered the ravages of the enemy's claws, managed to raise great and godly kids whose lives were beautiful, fruitful, and rich. All because the moms and dads said, "This is where it stops. This is where the enemy backs off. Not my kids." The reward for such godly parents cannot be measured, nor will their children fully realize this side of heaven what their parents did, and gave up, and agonized over, and endured so that their children could enjoy such a wonderful life.

Your ministry may be to lead your co-workers to Jesus, to contribute time and money and prayer to your church and community needs. But you are a FULL PARTNER in the Kingdom work, without which the "base runners" and long-distance sprinters could not win. ALL of us, in that sense, are in full-time ministry.

You know, sometimes this race – this game – gets discouraging for us. It is hard to keep your faith and witness before a Christless world that tries to tear down our morals, our integrity, our hope.

And we must never forget that we have a very real enemy on the other side of this game. And Satan knows he can't win. He can only get *us* to quit. That's the victory he gets if he can get it.

Our victory isn't in the score but in the refusal to quit the game. As long as you hit the ball, feeble as that hit may be, or run a base, or jump over an obstacle, YOU WIN. Isn't that marvelous?

A young girl at camp came to the nurse's office, all scraped up and bruised from a kickball fall. She was in tears from the pain. The camp director said, "Well, was it worth it?" Yeah!" she replied through tears and a mile-wide grin. "I scored four points!"

Stay in the game. Keep scoring on the enemy. Your part – in the game or on the sides – matters more than you know.

3 A CAGE

I love my bird. Though he is currently residing with family, I see him once or twice a week. He knows me. He's just a sweet bit of God's love stuck into some feathers and a beak. Cockatiels are so cool, especially if you get them as babies being hand raised. One of my best friends and our band drummer knew I was looking for one. He found one. He was one of several born in the office of a real estate lady he knew.

The only problem was that he was the runt of the bird litter. The bigger birds were picking on him. Perfect. I'd love every little feather of him.

Gandalf Graybeard. He was fun, annoying, sweet, needy, smart. Somehow, he learned the theme to the Andy Griffith theme song in two weeks of sitting and watching it with me. It wasn't perfect, he got stuck on parts of it, but we could duet on it pretty well. I didn't try to teach him the Twilight Zone theme, but apparently, he picked it up during the few episodes I watched once a month. Smart. Happy.

One time I saw him chirping and swinging back and forth like there was nothing better in the world. Then I heard a bang! The poor little guy had gotten so rambunctious that he had slipped off the swing and slipped off the perch and ended up dazed and feathers ruffled at the bottom of the cage. I felt bad but he wasn't hurt and he had this look like, "What happened?" in his eyes, and I laughed till tears came to my eyes. Oh, Gandalf. What an innocent, pure bit of joy you are! And you even learned to say your name. Well, sort of. "Gan-dolf gray BURRRD!" Good enough for me.

He was a real comfort to me. If you live long enough, you begin to chart some significant losses. Jobs, ministries, churches, but then people. Death. As you age, your tribe starts to depart—first, parents, then siblings, cousins, sometimes even your spouse. Then, inevitably, eventually, you. It's hard. It hurts.

My losses began a little early in life. By the time Gandalf came around, I'd lost mom and pop, all the Grands, all the aunts and uncles, and even some cousins. I felt lonely. I felt left behind. It was really starting to bother me, even after all these years of walking with Jesus. Gandalf took the edge off of the losses, somehow. Hard to be sad with his antics going on 24/7. I was grateful for him and for my family and church friends.

Still, I was beginning to have more and more of those "I'm probably next" moments, and it bothered me that dread was starting to replace my younger "Take me anytime Jesus!" rapture-ready enthusiasm. I had big regrets, wasted years, and a growing sense of what little I had done for Jesus in my short life. "God, I don't understand death. It scares me, really. I hate to admit it, but it's true. I know what Your Word says about eternal life, and I believe every word. But I'm spooked. I'm an orphan. Can you talk to me about death? Thank you." That was my simple and soon forgotten prayer.

I got busy, a great escape for me, always.

Church family camp was coming up, and as a youth pastor, I had lots of things to do to get ready. Messages to prepare, calls to make, packing camp stuff (where is that raggedy old sleeping bag? Can't believe it made it another year…) Packing snacks and packing up Gandalf were usually the last things I took care of before a trip. I always dreaded packing my feathered buddy into a carrying cage and trotting him off to his other family for the duration. It was always like dealing with a little kid. "We're going to the doctors." "I don't WANNA!" or, SCREECH, SCREECH SCREECH! in Galdalfspeak. I had started to wear gloves to take him from a big cage to little because as much as Gandalf loved me, he wasn't budging without a battle. And he could seriously bite.

I got him packed up in a quick hurry, delivered him to his weekend caregivers, and hurried back to do my final packing for the trip.

I got home, rushed into the large bedroom where my clothes and suitcase (and Gandalf) were kept, and the Holy Spirit stopped me at the door, and my eyes gazed upon the eternal moment I'd prayed for.

In the middle of the room, there stood Gandalf's now-empty cage, and the beautiful picture of his cage door standing open.

Galdalf was gone. (Though he'd merely moved houses.)

I immediately understood, and tears of gratefulness came from my eyes.

"Thank You…"

Death, for the believer, is simply freedom from a cage.

All these years, we are stuck in a broken vessel, destined to break until it is no longer repairable.

Paul spoke of this: "For we know that if our earthly house, this tent, is destroyed, we have a building from God, a house not made with hands, eternal in the heavens. For in this we groan, earnestly desiring to be clothed with our habitation which is from heaven, if indeed, having been clothed, we shall not be found naked. For we who are in this tent groan, being burdened, not because we want to be unclothed, but further clothed, that mortality may be swallowed up by life." (2 Corinthians 5:1-4) Not loss of life – but more life. "I go to prepare a place for you." Not orphaned…but leaving our earthly cage to enter a house made especially for us by His loving hands.

Death is freedom from our fleshly cage, released to fly to our forever Home.

4 A BRAZIL NUT

Bible School was the most significant faith venture of my young life. The call on my life for ministry – and to go to this specific Bible School – was as certain to me as my salvation.

I just had to pay for it. There were no scholarships. A few of my hoity-toity California theological brethren would probably call it a po-dunk Bible School. It didn't matter. I was under orders, and I was *going*.

There was some snobbery among Christian academics. There were respected and approved seminaries. Then there were Bible schools from "the other side of the tracks." The one God chose for me was considered the latter at the time.

My Bible School wasn't huge; it wasn't even credentialed or accredited yet. But it had some of the most solid, mature, anointed teachers anywhere. And while cemeteries (seminaries) all over were downplaying and tearing down the Bible (higher and lower criticism) and sending out ministers who had largely lost their faith in the Word of God, this school put the Word of God first. And faith.

So, being that I knew the call, I also knew I'd have to "faith it" through my first semester, not having the money to pay my way through. Miraculously, God had provided exactly what I needed to go – and one month's rent and food.

My schedule was full. I was a bit in shock, being a California to Texas transplant, but I adjusted. I found a couple of temporary jobs, paid some rent, bought some food, and I made it, sometimes day to day. Sometimes it was close. Sometimes there were just cans of collard greens (look it up) and the favorite college standby – soup – to eat.

A handful of folks back home knew I was "faithing my way" through that semester. And at odd times, I would get stamps, sunflower seeds, cookies, cinnamon sticks (a strange personal addiction I was known for) a note of encouragement, and even an occasional cash gift or check. They were never much, but they came at just the right time and were preparing me for the faith life I would enter when I went into full-time ministry a short two years later.

But, admittedly, I sweat it out. I would read the biographies of great men and women of God who lived by faith and felt both encouraged and personally lacking. George Mueller had an orphanage, and his biography told story after story of miraculous last-minute intervention of provision for the children of his orphanage. I'd read it wistfully and say, "God, I want to be like him," and then sadly, "I'm not like him…" My faith was small. But it was growing. And God made sure I was in the perfect place for that faith to grow. I got to watch specific financial needs met right down to the exact need time and time again and occasionally extra – "Handfuls on purpose," as one of our teachers Sister Pauline Parham called those extras. (Ruth 2:16)

Other times, the brook got pretty dry. It was then that I took refuge in stories of Elijah and the cloud like a man's hand, the loaves and fishes, and others. Sometimes I just said, "I trust You," and provision would come. Other times, in my youth and personal insecurity, I'd say, "God, how come it doesn't work for me?" when I ran out of provision. And then, the provision would come. "If we believe not, He remains faithful; He cannot deny Himself." (2 Timothy 2:13). God was always true. God always provided, whether my "faith" was strong or weak! He was true to His Word!

I was learning slowly, but surely.

One day, the "big test" came.

I was out of *everything*.

Not even jingling coins in my pocket. Not one can of collard greens.

And my roommate was gone.

I was stuck. I'd been here before. But *this* time, I wasn't going to whine and ask God what I was doing wrong in my faith – no way!

I found a Brazil nut. One lonely, solitary Brazil nut. The moment of truth had arrived.

I sat down at my tiny apartment desk, opened my Bible for my morning devotional, raised the Brazil nut, thanked God for what I was about to receive, cracked it open, put it in my mouth, bit down – and broke my tooth.

The moment of truth…

The devil snickered. "I GOT him!" "Where is your God NOW?" Satan always tries to use that line. I think he watched too many Edward G. Robinson movies. "Where is your God nooooowwwww?"

I took a deep breath, extracted the broken tooth from my mouth. I stood up, grabbed my Bible, two study books and my Strong's concordance (now I know why they called it a Strong's back then. It weighed like ten pounds. You can carry it, or your Bible, but not both. Something will be dropped. Or pulled.) Nevertheless, I grabbed them all. I stood up and said, "God, I am not going to let the devil win. You're my provider!" And I decided to shove it in the devil's face by – since he decided to break my tooth – going out by the pool, and (wait for it) study the Bible!

I know the devil wasn't shaken, but I believe God smiled on His little lamb's bleating attempt to face down the big bad wolf, the lamb not having any idea the bruising that was actually awaiting the wolf.

It took me about twenty minutes to fully accept that, as I had gone over to the campus pool and sat in the big chair and settled in to study hard – that it was March in Dallas, it was about 40 degrees and the winds were bitterly blowing. And I was freezing. Feeling foolish and defeated, I grabbed my books and notebook with my now numb fingers and dejectedly walked back to my apartment.

There was something outside my apartment door.

Two bags, filled with groceries.

And a card.

I quickly opened the door to my apartment and brought them inside. I opened the card:

"The Lord told us to bring these to you two days ago, but we forgot. Please forgive us for being late! God bless you!"

There was a $50 bill in the envelope. Which, back then, was more like $300.

Jesus, thank You!!! I barely knew this couple. And they did not know my situation. Only Jesus could have known.

I feel like that's the moment the devil got slapped a good one. As he always is, when he intends hurt, discouragement, fear, and doubt, and Jesus steps in and does what He always does – provides, loves, blesses.

My faith grew by miles, thanks to that little Brazil nut. It was my mustard seed. And what an incredible harvest of miracles followed over the years, and continue to this day. God is always enough!

5 FORGIVE

I was new to church, not having gone since I was about ten. After I was saved at 15, I was invited to a church by some of my new friends who were my age and had just gotten saved as well.

It was a little church in Topanga Canyon, California. I was naïve and just wanted to worship this wonderful Jesus I had just met with my friends, unaware that this congregation was an established, settled group, and we completely unsettled them. (Why isn't anyone else raising their hands when they worship here?" I wondered to myself.)

It was my first real exposure to the church, the good, the bad, and the ugly. I met my spiritual mom there – good. The pastor asked me to leave – bad.

I saw the ugly when, every Sunday, a man with a suit and tie and a 50's style hat (think gangster movie) stood at the exit and passed out anti-Jewish literature. Yes, it happened at church.

I'm not sure what kind of influence this man had in that church, but the pastor did not say a word and did not stop him.

I was horrified when I took one of his little papers and read something like this:

"We don't have a conference of wolves and sheep. We don't have a conference of communists and Americans. We don't have a conference of snakes and children. SO

WHY DO WE HAVE A CONFERENCE OF CHRISTIANS AND JEWS??

It went on to write about how wrong it was that Christ-killers were in alliance with Christian groups.

This was the scariest man I'd ever met as a Christian so far. And he was there EVERY SUNDAY.

I met this nice elderly man named Augie Luft at the church, a kindly gentleman with a twinkle in his eye and full of gentle love for Jesus, and for people.

And he was a Jewish believer.

The astonishing happened one Sunday as I was going out the door behind Augie, he came face to face with this Nazi monster in Christian clothes, and looked him in the eye, said, "God bless you" to the steely-eyed man in the hat.

Then I saw it. A number tattooed on Augie's arm. My world stopped as I witnessed a kind of grace I had never seen before – or since.

Augie, I learned, survived Auschwitz, but most of his family did not.

And here was an evil man bringing into the house of God the same evil that had numbered – and murdered – his family and friends.

If anyone had a "right" to hate, it was Augie. And none of us would have blamed him.

Instead, he followed the example of the lamb of God who said, "Father, forgive them, for they know not what they do" and extended mercy to this wretched hateful soul.

It changed my life instantly. Never again would I not forgive, and many ugly things were to come to me over the years – unfair, hurtful, devastating things, almost all of them at the hands of believers. (And yes, I have hurt others and prayed to be forgiven.)

But it's not that I'm a super saint, and I have worked *hard* to let go of some wounding that was brutal, satanic and sometimes quite deliberate.

But I could never get Augie's face – and that number – and that moment – out of my mind and heart.

If he could forgive, how could I not, instead choosing to be cold, vindictive, and unforgiving? So much of my struggle seemed so petty in comparison to the weight this mighty man of God in a frail little Jewish body had borne.

"I'll forgive, but I'll never forget!"

"You don't know how evil they are!"

"You don't understand how badly they hurt me!"

Sound familiar?

"Father, forgive them; they know not what they do," said the Crucified.

"God bless you," said the numbered, hated Jewish man shining with the love of Jesus.

GREGORY R REID

It's easy for us to talk a good game about loving people.

In one eternal moment, Augie demonstrated love in a way that would haunt, convict, and instruct me for the rest of my life.

May I attain to be even a little like that gentle, godly man.

28

6 MIRACLE IN THE MAYHEM

I am writing this in the midst of a kind of chaos, violence, and uncertainty I have not seen for many years. Following a pandemic lockdown, we are now watching a racial meltdown once again.

I, like many others, am trying to hold steady and not be moved to the right or to the left, but I'm asking to be moved only by what moves His heart. It is frustrating and difficult, and for myself, I am always second-guessing what I am doing or saying, wanting to make sure I am standing strong, speaking scripturally, and that I am in obedience to His Will.

This morning was difficult. I was tired. The night before had been a battle, and sleep had been restless.

I read a few verses in Jeremiah, then decided to watch a live video of a young black woman and her small crew bringing the truth and life and power of Jesus right inside the hotspot in Seattle. I watched for almost an hour, listening, praying…captivated by the boldness and the presence of God in their prayers and their words.

After that hour, I shut it off. "God, what can I do in the midst of all this mess? I'm doing what I can, but I want to do everything you ask…"

My cell phone rang. I *never* answer it unless I know who it is. Except this time. "Hello?" I asked. "Hello, did you call me? I don't recognize your number." I heard the voice of an elderly black woman. "No, ma'am," I replied. "I didn't call." "Is your number x.x.x.x.x.x.x.?" she asked. "Yes, it is." "Who are you?" she asked. I said, "I'm Gregory Reid." "I don't know you." "Can I ask your name?" I asked, and she gave me her name. "Well," I said, "Even though I didn't call, may God bless you and give you a wonderful week." "God bless you too," she said. Everything stopped. "Ma'am, can I ask you if there's anything you need prayer for?" "Yes, you can, thank you. Pray that I can get through this mess that's going on right now. I'm 87, and my health is bad. Please pray for that too." In a moment, everything changed. I begin to pray for her. I am weeping through my prayers. She is praying too. Jesus showed up. After a little more prayer, she told me she was the daughter of a Baptist minister. We talked for several minutes. I told her I was a minister, and she asked me where. I told her I had a home fellowship and also went to two other churches when I could. She told me she would be praying for God to help me.

Suddenly, I understood.

I didn't make that call.

Jesus did.

For the next few minutes, I poured out my heart to this dear lady through my tears. "You may have thought God is done with you, that you are not even sure why God keeps you here," I said. "It's because God needs you in this hour. We need our mothers and fathers in the faith. You are the prayer warriors. You are the ones who know how to pray. You are the generals of the faith! Ma'am, I'm asking you to pray for me. Pray for my generation that is so lost. Pray for the young people that are lost. Without a miracle, this nation isn't going to survive all of this." I don't remember most of the conversation, but what I can tell you is, Jesus had made a phone call to both of us. Me, wondering if I can even make a tiny dent in the darkness out there, her, maybe feeling alone and wondering how she was going to get through the next day. Jesus took two hands from different colors and brought them together, and He was in our midst. We are not divided. Jesus – and only Jesus – has made us one family, of one blood. It was a miracle. But that's who Jesus is. That's what He does. That's what He is still doing.

Centuries ago, a man named Philip was preaching to a multitude. The Spirit told him to go down to a road far from where he was, to a desert road. He saw a black man in a chariot, and the Spirit told Philip to join him. The man was an assistant to Queen Candace of Ethiopia. He was reading Isaiah. Philip asked him if he knew what he was reading. "How can I, unless someone explains it?" the man said. So, Philip explained the Word to him and told him about Jesus. They came upon some water. "What's keeping me from getting baptized?" The man asked. "If you believe with all your heart, you can." "I believe that Jesus Christ is the Son of God," the man answered, and so Philip baptized him, and when they came up, God snatched Philip away and put him on another assignment. The man didn't see Philip anymore, but he went on his way rejoicing.

This morning I experienced a miracle only Jesus could do. It was much like this story in Acts. I made no call. But across the states, Jesus was calling us both.

And the message was clear.

As I told my new friend, this mother in the Lord, Jesus cared so much about her that he had me, a flawed and broken servant of the Lord - states away - answer a call from an unknown number, and we spent the next fifteen minutes with Jesus together, because He wanted her to know He loves her, and she still is needed of Him in this critical time. But the call was two-way. Jesus used her to call me, not knowing who I was. I needed the encouragement. I needed to see Jesus' hand at work today. I needed to remember what this is all about.

He wanted me to know He heard my prayer that I could actually make a difference in all the awful we're going through.

There was no black or white. There was no racial anything—just one bond in the blood of our crucified Savior.

And *that* is the answer to it all. Jesus is.

When you and I are in Jesus, nothing else matters but Jesus and His love and His kingdom. And if you and I are in Jesus, we will realize He is alive and well and waiting for us to be His hands extended to a lost and hurting world. People think this answer is simplistic but it is not. What the world needs is Jesus. He is the only one that can heal the broken, tormented, angry hearts on every side and in every person, young, old, Hispanic, Chinese, black, white, or anyone else. In Christ, there is no Jew nor Greek. In Christ, there is no racial divide.

Jesus, through tears and gratefulness, I thank you – you are still doing miracles. Jesus, please let us be vessels of your grace, your truth, and your good news of healing, deliverance, and reconciliation through the cross of your dear Son. "...that God was in Christ, reconciling the world unto Himself." (2 Cor. 5:19)

All they need to do is surrender in broken repentance at that cross, be cleansed of their sins, and He will change their lives forever.

But how will they hear without a preacher? And that is me, and that is you.

Jesus, give us holy boldness, broken compassion, and the power of Your Word and Your Spirit to reach all those who are in need of your love. All we need is to come to Your cross and surrender our all.

Believer, this is for you. If you just yield, stay of a broken, contrite heart and let Him, you can be the arms and heart of Jesus to this lost world.

And if you are one of our elderly that has felt useless, discarded, purposeless, please hear me. We need you now more than ever. Pray for us. God is listening. God has not forgotten you. You have proof of that in this little message I offer. Without your prayers, we cannot fight well; we cannot be who we need to be in this hour. We need you.

Jesus called me this morning too. I needed to see His hand at work, and as much as my phone called this precious saint I did not know, she called me back, and God connected our hearts across all the divides of human sin and brokenness, and for that moment, I felt I had touched heaven with a friend. I am renewed. I am restored. And I can't wait to see the miracle God does next!

How about you?

7 JUST A VESSEL

There were four kinds of messages I heard growing up as a believer.

One was the completely unanointed, cringeworthy, totally flesh message – messages that were completely unbiblical or preached out of anger, or frustration, or the worst one, someone else's sermon – downloaded and printed and preached as if it was their own.

Two was the teaching message – usually a bit dry, good solid stuff but a bit hard to sit through.

Three was the mixture – a message cobbled together from jokes, cute expressions, and helpful social lessons but somehow then moves into a Holy Spirit place where His Word overcomes their word, and He is able to work powerfully despite the weak beginnings.

And four was the rare, from beginning to end, God-touched message that left you staggered and touched to the very core.

That fourth kind is pretty rare!

In the end, though, we are all just human vessels praying for God's touch on our attempts to bring Jesus to a hurting world.

That's hard in an age when people still look for Christian superstars to elevate and emulate. It's hard for the Christian leader that has flaws and hard for the followers who think they don't - or shouldn't - have them.

I'm not sure which of my Christian leaders, mentors, or pastors said this to me, but I am so glad they did: "At some point, I am going to let you down." Because I was prepared, when it happened, I wasn't shocked, and I didn't turn from Jesus. And I did not love them less for it. I actually loved them more because they told me beforehand, and they were willing to help me work through the hurt I felt initially, and even though they felt the pain of failing me, they were willing to keep walking with me if I overcame my disappointment and let them continue to speak into my life.

I am human, flawed, and sinful. I'm also called to ministry. So, I work hard to keep my sins at bay and crucified, get the flaws healed, keep my weaknesses from hurting others, and, well, there's nothing I can do about being human!

No one is more surprised than I am when God uses me in spite of it all.

Others occasionally struggle with that inevitable clash.

It was one of those nights when everything just went perfect – right church, wonderful people, great worship – and by the time I got up to preach, the groundwork had already been laid, the stage set. All I had to do was step up, open my Bible, and open my mouth and let God speak.

And speak, He did. It was one of those rare moments where I would have had to go back and listen to the message to see what I said.

I think all of us who are doing preaching ministry long for such moments when we simply step up and let the Lord speak through us. There is, for me, a moment when I start with notes in hand and begin to preach when at some point, the Holy Spirit just overcomes me, and the fire falls. Those moments are precious to me; it is that place where He just gently moves me aside and ministers through me, in spite of my human weaknesses, in spite of my fears or struggles before I get into the pulpit. I just sit back and let the Lord take me with Him, and I enjoy the ride.

This was that kind of night. I started slow, and within moments, that unction came, and it just poured out of me. People were saved that night. People were set free. It went longer than planned, but no one wanted to interrupt what God was doing. In a human sense, I had hit it out of the ballpark. In a Holy Spirit sense, I had simply gotten out of His way, and He did the rest.

Afterward, I was exhausted but happy, and the "afterglow" went on a long time as the pastors and I talked and prayed with people. I could have gone home to Jesus happy that night, so perfect it had gone.

As we were leaving, a group of people approached me. " Can you go have coffee with us?" "Sure," I agreed, a little reluctantly, simply because, well, here's the big reveal – I am extremely shy around people when I am not preaching. *Really* shy and *really* nervous. But I didn't want to say no, so off I went with them.

They were full of questions, and I did my best to answer them. The sometimes-awkward silent moment between conversation caused my nervous side to finally take over. I did what I had done for years – usually for youth – and a thing that always caught their attention and that they turned around later and did for others. It's called "the worm." I took a straw and scrunched the paper down the straw into a tight little wad. Then I got a little water in a straw, dripped it onto the paper, and voila! Straw uncurls and grows and stretches out like a paper worm. Fun trick. For kids.

The silence caused me to go to the next step, which was to tell a kind of lame joke. "What did the snail on the back of the turtle say? Whee!!!" My youth group liked it.

No so much for these folks. I'm not really sure how I expected them to react; in fact, I did it as a nervous, "Well now what do we talk about" act. They just looked at me, horrified.

"We thought you were a man of God!" one said with a bit of disgust at my excellent worm trick and my feeble joke.

Before I thought about it, the words were out: "You mean that guy back there at the church? That was Jesus working through him. Now it's just me. This is just me."

I know it was disappointing to them to hear that. But it was in the middle of the superstar Christian era in the church, and everyone was glorifying men and women and anointed prophets and influential apostles and following them, quoting them, elevating them.

And so many times, those people fell into gross sin or excess, leaving spiritual wreckage in their wake.

I have never had any delusions about God using me. There is nothing in me that is special or dynamic or amazing. From the very first time I preached to ten special needs kids to the time a year later I preached to 1000 people – I knew it was God and God alone who made me a worthy vessel of His Word.

Kathryn Kuhlman used to say, "It's not vessels of gold He is seeking, it's not vessels of silver. It's yielded vessels.

My constant prayer has been to be yielded, with all of my heart and in all of my humanity, to the Holy Spirit and allow Him to use me as He pleased.

Paul's words resonated with me from the first time I read it and continue to be a shining light in the path ahead of me in ministry: "We have this treasure in earthen vessels, that the excellency of the power may be of God, and not of us." (2 Cor. 4:7)

Just a vessel! Just a container for His Spirit. Let it be so that no matter what God does, it is clear that it was God alone who did it, and we just unworthy servants of His Kingdom.

I have not stopped making straw worms. And I have never given anyone the delusion that I had anything to do with whatever God has chosen to do in and through me. Knowing those things, far from proving that we are not men and women of God, demonstrates that we are in the end, simply vessels of clay that are honored and humbled to be a vessel for the Spirit of the Living God – and happy to just be "us" when the work is done.

8 CINDERS

Cinders was a fairly nice restaurant in my town. I had moved to El Paso that year, and one night a handful of the guys I had met at the church college group and I decided to go there to eat. We couldn't afford this place very often, so it was something we really looked forward to. They were great guys, full of Jesus and full of themselves, full of laughter and passion and life. I loved their company. I could be myself, which, as a young minister, was very difficult because you're always expected to be "on." I could just be myself with these guys and trust that they wouldn't treat me any different or throw it back in my face later and say, "You think you're so righteous, I remember when you…" People in ministry know what I mean. So I felt especially blessed to have this "band of brothers" to travel on this part of the battlefield with me.

And getting a night off, just to hang out, just to eat and joke and act like young men, well, that was a rare treat for me. Called to ministry early and started at 18, I was already accustomed to the battle and travel and stress and the weariness that true ministry brings. I always looked forward to just a night out, you know, like "normal humans" do.

It was a great evening, relaxed, peaceful. Cinders had incredible steak and seafood, so we were in no rush to get through and get gone. We talked about school, friends, church stuff, Saturday Night Live skits. (Yes, it was a while ago, when it was actually funny.)

At last, they were getting ready to close, and we got up and paid the bill, and headed out for our cars. In the dimly lit parking lot, we saw a man leaning into a car and heard a woman screaming. We froze. He slammed the door, walked by us in a fury, cursing the woman, so drunk he could barely stand up. He stormed back into the restaurant. I assumed he was going to make a call.

Alarmed, we cautiously walked up to the car to see if the woman, who was still crying and screaming, was injured or needed help. "Are you OK?" I asked. "NO, I'M NOT!" she screamed. "AND HE'S GOT A GUN!" "OK guys," I said quietly, "I think we need to go." I figured I could go call the police from across the street. We turned to head back to our cars, and the man came out of the restaurant, still full of fury, and he's headed right for my three friends and I. "Why don't you take those guys on if you're such a big man, HUH?" The lady screamed at him out of the car window. He was up for the challenge, and I suddenly felt my three friends take a few steps back, leaving him and me on a direct collision course. He had a gun. I knew this was real. But I had no time to think. I could only whisper, "Help me, Jesus."

"OK," the guy screamed. "I'm gonna take you on first!" He yelled and pulled back his fist in a split second. In another split second, with clear, bold words, I said, "Mister, you need Jesus!"

Everything stopped. I watched as his fist froze in midair, and it began to shake. He looked at his fist and looked at me, unable to make his fist move. Then he broke down and began to sob. "I know I need Jesus! My wife does too! Please, please, come home and pray with us!" I went up and put my hand on his shoulder and looked him in the eyes. "Of course, we will," I said, and we did. We went to their house and spent the better part of three hours praying with them and trying to help them patch up their damaged marriage.

As believers, we often think about what it must be like to really suffer for the faith like so many do around the world. I think it is good to think about it. There is always the thought of, "what will I do when danger faces me, when my life is threatened, or my family's life? Will I be able to stand for Jesus, no matter the cost, no matter the pain?"

My little story does not even begin to touch on the real danger or the real suffering of believers around the world. But still, for me, it was a moment that I had long thought about. I can talk brave when preaching, in times of peace, when there is no threat, and I am safe. But what if my life were threatened? What then? Would I run, would I beg for mercy, would I ever, God forbid, deny my Lord to spare my life?

I can, like everyone, only depend on His grace. As Corrie Ten Boom's father told her as a little girl, "When do you get your ticket for the train? Only when we arrive at the station. You do not need it until then." So it is with the grace we will need to pass through any such trial.

The night before, if I had been told I would be confronted with someone who had a gun, I would have had a great deal of fear. But in the very moment when it became a real-life threat, instead of fear, I felt the power and love of God speak out of me, and God turned a threat into a life-changing moment for Jesus to heal and set free.

I remember David Wilkerson telling the story of walking through the mean streets of New York and seeing a group of older gang members beating up on a little kid at the baseball field. He said he did not hesitate but instead ran into the danger, picking up a baseball bat along the way, and ran towards the gang, screaming at them like a madman to let the kid go. They did.

God will give us exactly what we need at the moment we need it. Do you believe that? Perhaps, like all of us, you have fears. God doesn't condemn. Like David, we say, "When I am afraid, I will trust in the You." (Psalm 56:3)

The story is told of the great early church leader Polycarp, the bishop of Ephesus after John the Beloved. He had one fear. Fire.

The Romans pursued him; believers hid him; they finally caught him. He was sentenced to be burned at the stake.

But what did he do? Was he begging for his life, ready to deny Jesus to spare him from his greatest fear?

It is told that he asked permission to make a meal for the soldiers that held him before his execution, in a last astonishing act of God's love reaching out to the lost.

And when he was to be bound, he asked not to be, saying, "Leave me thus, for He who gives me power to endure the fire, will grant me to remain in the flames unmoved even without the security you will give by the nails" And He remained unbound, and Polycarp died without fear, with arms raised in worship.

Do not fear. My small encounter showed me that God is with us every moment, every second, and no matter what the fear we have or the danger we face, He will be with us. Not only that, He will use every moment to show His power and love and glory, no matter what the circumstance, if we just walk every moment in obedience to Him.

GREGORY R REID

9 BROKEN

I've never been very good at avoiding objects. In fact, I've got a bit of a reputation for, well, being a bit of a self-hazard. My track record of injuries was so evident that my youth group once suggested bubble wrapping me before going on any kind of an outing.

We even kept an injury count on one youth mission trip : seventeen injuries in a week.

I mean, how do you cut yourself on *ice?*

During a Walmart run, I sat in the van in the sweltering Dallas summer heat and humidity, waiting for the kids and other leaders to return from shopping. One of the middle school kids got back first and jumped in the back seat with his newly acquired action toy.
"Here, open this OK?" he said, shoving it up to me between the seats. "Sure," I dutifully replied, taking out my trusty pocketknife.

I think one of the most singularly most horrible inventions in history is the hard plastic shell packaging that they put around nearly everything – toys, office supplies, doggie treats. (Which answered the question, "How do you drive your dog crazy? Answer: just give him the package and don't open it.")

I think one of my favorite memes was a picture of a pair of scissors in a hard plastic wrapping with the title, "Satan has left you a present." *So* much truth…

So here I was, using my knife to open his toy, and….yeah, the knife slipped and went right into my

47

thumb. Deep. I saw stars. I scrambled for napkins and towels to stanch the bleeding. "Can you hurry *up*?" the boy impatiently demanded from the back, unaware that his loving youth pastor had potentially sacrificed his thumb so he could have his toy. "CAN.YOU. PLEASE. WAIT," I said tensely, praying I didn't go completely Joan Crawford Kabuki Wire Coathanger on him.

Happily, he got his toy. And I survived. Youth battle scars!

Even though youth ministry did increase the possibility of getting injured more frequently, accidents would happen to me regardless.

Mom always said, "Haste makes waste," and I think half of my issue is that my brain is always in overdrive, and my feet are usually in a "hold on a minute, Sparky!" mode and can't keep up with the challenge. So my brain is already five feet ahead by the time it figures out because of the pain receptors screaming that I have, in fact, connected intimately with the couch – or as I like to call it, the Automatic Furniture Finder.

So enough background to my story, which if I were to go into full detail, would include falling off a ladder 20-feet onto cement, fracturing my arm in a skateboard accident at 45 (all I did was stand on it, and it immediately became a high-speed merry-go-round catapult to the ground), falling backward onto a boat and hitting my head on an engine, having a full pot of coffee poured down my back at a restaurant, and making salsa with Jalapenos without gloves. (My hand bones burned for three days.)

I had gone quite a while (as in, three months) without a mishap. Then one morning, I was coming down the stairs from my loft carrying a heavy glass dish that was about 2 feet long and required both hands. At the 4th step from the bottom, I heard a loud SNAP! My foot buckled, and I went headlong down the last four steps.

I had put my hands in front of me to cushion the fall and ended up sprawled in the narrow hallway. The snap had, apparently, been a bone in my foot.

The next few hours were spent trying to convince myself that it wasn't broken, counter-arguing that a sprain would hurt more, and then finally ending up at the ER. Dancer's fracture, they called it. I'd never heard of it, and I don't dance. But I did hurt. A *lot*.

The result was a soft cast and crutches for three weeks and having to move my sleeping arrangements from upstairs to a more safe place downstairs. I hated the restraints, but I was thankful it wasn't worse.

In fact, it would have been a lot worse except for God's intervention.

I am not sure when it occurred to me, being that I was a bit traumatized for the next few hours and a couple of days, that I had been carrying a potentially lethal heavy glass tray when I fell. If I had fallen with it, my wrists would have instinctively been extended to break my fall, and I would have shattered the glass with them and possibly bled out before I could get help.

I found the glass tray. It was almost ten feet away from the stairs on the floor, intact and placed almost perfectly.

There is no human hand that did that. There was no human possibility that without remembering it, I had deftly tossed the 3-pound tray as I realized I was falling and managed to do so in such a way that it landed like a feather, unbroken.

I believe in angels. I know some people get a bit crazy on the angel thing, but when you know God sent one or two to intervene, you can't help but glorify and thank God for the miracle. Jesus is with us. And He is quick to dispatch his angels to help us when we need them.

I've slowed down a bit since then, tried to watch where I am going more diligently. But I have a complete assurance that when I am in trouble or danger, Jesus is there with me. And although we are not always protected from injury, illness, or suffering, I have an absolute assurance that He has surrounded us with those who are assigned to our care and that nothing we go through is without His loving presence and ability to endure.

10 IN THE WAITING

I had just gotten out of Bible School, and I spent months agonizing about what to do next. I knew God had called me. My heart was full of fire and passion for lost, hurting people – especially kids. So at 20, I spent most of my days walking into the hills behind my parent's house in Sylmar, CA, and sat on a sandstone rock and prayed – prayers of confusion, frustration, asking for direction.

Mostly, I heard nothing back.

The calling burned in me. I knew I was born for Kingdom Work. But how did I get there? How could I get doors to open? I was an unknown person and was on nobody's radar. But I knew God knew my address. So I waited and prayed for him to track me down and put me in the Kingdom field.

Thankfully, my parents weren't going to throw me out. But Mom started hinting and nudging that I needed to do, well, something. Anything. She had finally realized I wasn't going to outgrow this "religious phase" she thought I was going through when I first got saved. She and Pop had even helped me get through my first year of Bible school. But she probably didn't want her son turning into some guru sitting on a rock in the back of the house and communing with nature...

So, she not too subtly placed the want ads under my cereal bowl each morning, with jobs circled she thought I could get.

But I didn't want a "job."

I also didn't want to be seen as the lazy bad Christian example, so I started checking out those jobs.

I landed the first job I applied for in Hollywood, at a mail-order clothing store. It was perfect. I was excited! I went home and told my parents, reported on time the next day. I was sent into the back room to work, where I was shown how to package and ship jeans – and pornography. The job lasted exactly five minutes, long enough for me to walk out the door.

The next day, I got another job. It was a lamp factory. Easy work. They hired me, and within half an hour, I was completely covered with a rash – probably an allergic reaction to asbestos.

I was frustrated, as were my parents. But for me, it was confusion: Why did God have me go through a year of Bible School if I wasn't going to do anything with it?

"Why don't you come up and do some street ministry with me while you're waiting?" my pastor, Rev. Glenn Adkins, asked after church that next Sunday.

I had been at Glenn's church for three years. It was a tiny little country church nestled in the center of Topanga Canyon, California. It was the home of actors and ex-actors, burnt-out rock stars, drug dealers, witches, Satanists, psychopaths, people running from their lives, people running from the law.

I was to leave this particular church a few years before because my friends and I were not welcome. We were "Jesus people" kids, and the church did not want us there.

I found another church (thanks to my spiritual mom, who wouldn't let go of me and insisted I go somewhere) a year or so later. It was a Foursquare church, and the pastor, Carl Burns, was the coolest guy. He must have been in his late fifties then, and he had longish silver hair and rode a chopped Harley. He was cooler than the youth pastors who were there when I was there! I was kind of a rebel that wanted to set the world on fire for Jesus, and he was a conservative evangelical who sometimes called me out for being a rebel. I remember we would fight, and then apologize, and then lock horns again, rinse, repeat…but mainly, I felt very loved by this man and this church.

In fact, one of my first memories of actually feeling loved by a pastor happened there. I remember the first week I went to a Sunday night service. I was still kind of sensitive because of my last church rejection. But the presence of God was in this little church, and I went up after the message and the prayer meeting and just sat on the floor cross-legged, longing for God's touch. The worship music played softly in the background. As I sat there with my head bowed, I felt the gentle hands of this pastor on my shoulder and head, and he quietly prayed through tears, "O God, please help this young man, touch him, Jesus, fill him with Your love!" I felt so much love at that moment, and I grew to love him because of his compassion for the hurting.

I endured watching a difficult youth pastor removal, but I stayed. I went on two men's retreats with them and sat under Pastor Carl's fiery preaching. I loved this church.

So when I clearly heard the Lord tell me to return to the church I had been kicked out of, I objected vehemently. Why should I go back to the church that didn't want me there? So I didn't

Then the second week, the pressure was even stronger. Still, I dug my heels in. "I love this place. Surely this must be the devil trying to get me to leave," I reasoned.

The third week was the most miserable church service I'd ever been to. I felt…nothing. I felt disconnected. I couldn't wait to get out of there. I knew when I got home, it wasn't them…God was making the nest uncomfortable so I had to obey Him.

When I returned to the church I had left, there was a new pastor, Rev. Glenn Adkins.

Glenn was the perfect pastor/evangelist for that village. He was a big redneck guy from Bakersfield, California, and then Oxnard. He had a larger than life big huge booming Gospel/opera voice, and he was afraid of *nothing*. Most people loved him, a few hated him, but nearly everyone respected him.

When I went back, the church was down to a handful of people, mainly young couples, a few who were my age, and of course, my ever-faithful spiritual mother who had stuck to the church for decades through all the difficulties and changes.

Glenn tapped me for worship music along with another young lady from the church, and we did our best to lead the congregation every other Sunday. We truly were a small but very real family. Glenn was real. In fact, one rainy Sunday morning, just a few people showed up. We ended up in the kitchen, just praying, and when one of the men broke down crying and asked for prayer for his marriage, Glenn and all of us just surrounded him and prayed for him. That was church!

Glenn and his dear wife Frankie (who deserves triple saint awards for all she put up with in ministry!) and their little ones lived in the church. Glenn spent all day evangelizing, counseling, putting his life on the line for the sake of the call, and Frankie and the kids sacrificed as well.

It was a dangerous calling. He was the real deal.

So while I was waiting for my calling to begin, Glenn said, "Why don't you come up to the Canyon while you're waiting. I could use your help."

So I threw my guitar in the back of my car every day and made the 15 mile trip to the Canyon to hang out with Rev. Glenn. The first day I got there at about 3 pm, I picked up Glenn, and we drove the short distance down to "The Center," the ultimate hippie hangout of the time. We got out, and Glenn said, "Get your guitar and start singing." "What?" I said incredulously. "Start singing. I want to get some people over here." "I don't think I want to," I said, scared of people and no confidence in my singing abilities. "I'm your pastor, do what I tell you," he said, half-joking. I got the guitar out and sang a couple of songs I'd written. We got a crowd. And then he sang. When Glenn sang, you could hear it through the whole Canyon, I think. He had the clearest, operatic, Gospel voice I'd ever heard before or since, and when he sang, people paid attention whether they were believers or not.

I became Glenn's "associate" as he often introduced me, but I was more like his sidekick. I went with him everywhere, to coffee shops, to restaurants, to gritty, dangerous bars. I would spend hours just listening as Glenn shared Jesus with whoever would listen. Sometimes he asked me to share my own testimony with people. My frustration with not getting a ministry job or direction began to lessen as I got more involved with raw evangelism and street work. I listened. I learned. I got bolder.

One day I shared my testimony to several Canyon rats (as they were called, bikers, dealers, fugitives from the law etc.) One of them, a 6 foot something tall skinny tattooed guy with snaggled teeth and a mean demeanor, took a liking to me, and after that, if I was around, Gypsy was looking out for me. Gypsy had spent a year or two in hell in Vietnam, killed several people there, and apparently got out and killed some more. He was hiding from the law. Scary guy. But his heart was open to Jesus. I was glad to have his "protection" because I often shot my mouth off and ended up in trouble. One day I got in trouble with Trouble, one of the meaner Canyon Rats. We were in a bar, got our coffee, and sat at a table when Trouble and some friends came in, sat down, and started harassing us. They were stoned *and* drunk. Trouble started to mock God, and I got mad and lit into him. Bad idea. He immediately got up and pulled his fist back to take some of my teeth out, when suddenly a big old hand grabbed Trouble's hand and squeezed it until I was afraid I'd hear bones crunching. "Are you trying to mess with my *friend*, Trouble? Are you? Because Greg's my *friend!*" The look of fear on Trouble's face was priceless. "No, no, Gypsy, I swear! He's your friend? I'd never hurt him! Gypsy let go, and Trouble extended his hand. "If you're Gypsy's friend, you're *my* friend, dude! Cool?" Very.

One time I was completely on my own in one of the more dangerous bars and got into a conversation with a man in his early thirties who was getting completely drunk with friends. "You're the religious guy, aren't you?" he said, looking at me. I nodded, and for the next half hour, we engaged in a very real conversation about Jesus. I am always reluctant to have those conversations with people when they are drunk, knowing they may well forget all of it and me by the next morning. But this felt different. His friends were not happy about this conversation and were about to drag him away. "Thanks, man," he said, and hugged me. I was – by God's foresight – prepared, as I had already taken out a short bit of literature about God's love and how to find salvation, and as he hugged me, I managed to quickly slip it into his jean jacket pocket. Who knows? You never know.

But God does. That winter I got a letter from him. He'd moved to New York. He was alone and desperate. It was Christmas, and he was going to take his life. But he reached into his pocket for some matches and found my tract. "I read it. I gave my life to Jesus. Thank you, you saved my life." I was so grateful to God for that unexpected miracle!

For months I went with Rev. Glenn from place to place. We ministered to Bob Hite, "The Bear" from the 70's group Canned Heat, a backslidden Lutheran who was hooked on drugs and would come to church weeping for deliverance, then call us to come to pray for him, go into a demonic rage and throw us out. It broke my heart to learn that he died of an overdose shortly after that on the way to a gig at the Palomino bar in Van Nuys.

The 60's group Spanky and Our Gang also took a liking to Glenn, and we ended up sharing the Lord with some of them. They invited us to their gig at the Troubador – *the* music venue in Hollywood for rock bands – and they dedicated Larry Norman's "I Wish We'd All Been Ready" to Rev. Glenn. What an amazing time this was!

Larry Norman's song came into the picture again when Glenn was asked to sing at the Old Post Office, one of the rougher canyon bars. The owner really liked Glenn. "You've had nearly every kind of music in your bar. How about some Gospel?" Glenn asked. The owner thought it would be kind of novel, so he brought us in – Glenn and I and the young girl I sang with for worship at church and had a band with.

The reception was pretty harsh. There were mainly boos and "get off the stage!" through Glenn's opening Gospel opera song, then through our song. Once my friend and I were done, my friend and I went and sat on wooden benches that were next to the liquor room, which was right next to the outside of the bar. Just as Glenn started singing "I Wish We'd All Been Ready," there was a sound of an explosion and broken glass, and the entire building shook. My friend and I were nearly thrown off of the benches we sat on.

A drunk driver had come down the road, turned down into the Center, lost his brakes, and went slamming into the Post Office liquor room. His car came inches from going through my friend and I and likely killing us.

Once the commotion died down, Glenn resumed singing "I Wish We'd All Been Ready," and there was no sound as everyone listened. I think some people got saved that night!

Day after day, I would trek up the Canyon. I would sometimes not get home until 3-4 in the morning. This raised suspicion with my parents, who were concerned that I came home smelling of smoke and beer, and my explanation that I was doing ministry didn't cut it. It took a long call from Rev. Glenn to calm their fears.

"I feel like I'm supposed to minister in Hollywood," Glenn told me one day. "I'll show you the ropes," I told him. I'd been doing street evangelism there since I was about 17. He agreed. It was quite an education for Glenn, who thought he'd seen it all in the Canyon. "See her?" I'd whisper as we walked up the boulevard. "That's a prostitute." "How do you know? "I just do, trust me. See him?" "Yeah," Glenn answered. "He's a dealer. "Really?" "Yup. And see her? She's a he." I think I completely blew Glenn's mind. It opened up a new ministry for him, and for me for a while as well. We met a former assistant to a state senator who got radically saved and dragged us to meet everyone she could, from occultists to movie stars. Virginia was a 100-pound lady in her 70's that still smoked like a chimney even though she was saved (God would take care of that later!) One morning Virginia called me at 7 in the morning. (I don't – and never have – been able to handle mornings!) "Hi, darling!" she said in her gravelly, nicotine-bent voice, "I have a kid I picked up off the street. He needs Jesus. I'll be there in 15, and you can lead him to Jesus, OK doll?" I couldn't believe this lady. She was a true sheepdog. She brought the kid, and I did lead him to Jesus.

She brought Mr. Universe to lunch. He had it all and was making hundreds of thousands of dollars on things both illegal and not. He was totally uninterested in my testimony and Glenn's gospel presentation.

But Virginia called late that night: "You guys need to come down *right now*! My friend wants to receive Jesus!" So we made the late-night drive to Mr. Universe's house. He got radically saved and went on to become a well-known evangelist and, later, pastor of a major church in Southern California.

When the time came time came to take my first ministry job, I knew I was going to really miss this time with Rev. Glenn. And Rev. Glenn continued to blaze a trail for Jesus for years after that, not just in Topanga Canyon, but in Big Bear when he and his family moved there. I visited with Glenn and his dear wife, Frankie almost every time I was in Southern California.

The last time I saw Glenn was at the Jesus People Reunion event at Fuller Seminary. I could tell his health was declining, but it did not deter him from singing for the event in his powerful, booming, Spirit-filled voice for the hushed crowd. He remained the same. He continued to do street witnessing on the mountain where they lived, and continued to drive to L.A. and minister on skid row, pass out literature in front of the Playboy Club, and sing so loud you could hear him for a mile.

He got a Hoveround, which kept him mobile, and when he couldn't make it to L.A., he would pass out literature in his town and share Jesus with anyone who would listen. His homegoing was both a heartbreak and a celebration because we lost a true giant in the Kingdom when he went home. But what a legacy! Of all the men and women of God I have had the joy to know, this man stood tall in my life as a true Evangelist, 100% sold out, fearless, and real. He is sorely missed.

This story is longer than most of the rest in this book because I wanted to honor my "big brother" and his wife Frankie and their kids. They will probably smile at my lack of many details you only get from family, and maybe shed a tear because I know they miss him terribly.

Years later, it hit me: While I was waiting for the open door for my own ministry, I received the best, most priceless, genuine, dangerous, powerful training in evangelism I had ever had, ever would have, or ever will. In the waiting, God had prearranged for a big man named Rev. Glenn to give this green kid a front-row seat and front-line training beside the best. Thanks, big brother.

11 DISAPPOINTMENT

After almost six months out of Bible School, I was still agonizing before God about, "What's next?" I didn't' yet understand that the NOW I was in would be some of the most powerful days I would ever experience in ministry. One day Rev. Glenn told me, "I met this lady who is going to open up a live-in youth center in September. She's looking for live-in counselors. Maybe you could call her."

Grateful for the recommendation, I set up an appointment with Rev. Irene. We met late one morning in her office in Sylmar, CA. I walked in, we shook hands, we sat down, and the Holy Spirit showed up. She began crying. "You're the one God sent! You're hired!" she said. It was a profound moment. On the credentials of the Holy Spirit alone, she hired me, and I accepted. Details would follow!

The details: I would start at the end of September.

I would be a live-in counselor at Youth Defenders, a center for teens with drug-related and organic brain damage.

I had no training. I had no expertise whatsoever.

But no one wanted these kids. They were the throwaways. They were the forgotten ones. There weren't any really effective safety nets back then for kids like this. There were mental hospitals or foster homes, or the streets.

Rev. Irene had the heart to care for them. And after meeting them, so did I.

My first ever official sermon was preached to about ten mentally disabled or brain-damaged kids. And one 50-year old man who was emotionally a child.

I still count it as the most important message I ever gave. Not because of what I said. But because of who they were—greatly loved of God, mostly forgotten. Beautiful, lost, loved.

I moved in late September, along with my closest friend, who also had been hired. My job was to watch the kids, pray for them, and keep them safe. It was easy, and frustrating. I wanted them to be healed. But my old "you don't have enough faith" line I'd picked up from some Charismatic teachings didn't fit for some kids who didn't even understand the word "toilet."

That's when I had an early-on heart check in ministry. I heard the Lord say, "You only want them healed because they make you uncomfortable. And what if they are not healed? Will you still love them? Care for them?"

I was humbled and began to love them even more.

Dan was 50. He seemed normal compared with the young kids. And he wasn't a kid. He mainly just sat, and sighed, and said, "Oh, golly" over and over.

I asked Irene why he was there. She sadly told me Dan was homeless. His mother had died when he was ten, and he had simply stopped growing emotionally. She was his life. He never grew up.

I believe Jesus is the Great Healer – body, soul and spirit, mind, emotions, and heart.

"But if they are not healed…will you love them? Care for them?" "Comfort the feeble-minded." (1 Thess. 5:14) Jesus' love for Dan was immeasurable. I wanted to show him that somehow.

Andy was 13. Today, he would be labeled ADHD. Back then, he was labeled unmanageable. His father had recently died. His mom had completely fallen apart and became incapable of taking care of Andy. With no one else to care for him, she turned him over to our center. Andy was utterly alone. I took him under my wing to try to protect him.

Then there was Brad. He was 23 and completely demonized. He would grumble in strange words, curse and was utterly resistant to Jesus in every way.

I loved this calling! I would stay as long as God permitted.

We had a small chapel next to the dorms. I was going to sit out that Tuesday's service but felt compelled to go.

I was sleepy. I brought my Bible and was just grazing through Acts while Irene taught.

My eyes fell on a verse about Paul and Barnabas being laid hands on and being sent out.

Irene read the same verse that very moment.

Hm…

I faded back to Acts, not really listening to Irene. My eyes fell on another verse about Paul and Silas being commissioned…

Irene read the same verse.

I was now wide awake.

A third verse grabbed my attention about being sent out, and each time Irene would read the same verse after I read it. By this time, I was shaking under the Holy Presence of God. After one more verse, Irene stopped and said, "I can't continue. Greg, come up to the front. We need to lay hands on you and commission you."

I flew up to the front, almost eating carpet as I fell on my face under the power of God, trembling and praying and feeling a holiness that was almost terrifying. The sense of unworthiness I felt was overwhelming. I felt the hands of Irene and the elders on me, and I received the assurance of the Heavenly Call on my life and the commission to do the work of the Kingdom.

I arose exhausted and elated! I couldn't wait to see what was next.

I wouldn't have to wait long.

A few weeks after that on a Friday night, Brad was outside at midnight in his underwear, lying on his back, staring at the full moon, babbling in a demonic tongue, writing strange letters in a notebook. We prayed and bound whatever that was and got him back to his room.

The next day, Brad was harassing and threatening Andy. At one point, he got into his face, pointed a jabbing finger, and yelling, "You, you, *you*!"

I felt I had to do something. Andy needed protection, and Brad needed deliverance.

I called Irene repeatedly to no avail, leaving messages, and explaining the seriousness of the situation.

It escalated.

I finally took Brad into my office and prayed and cast a demon out of him. I believe he got free. I was so thankful!

The phone call came the next afternoon. "This is Irene." "Hi, I was trying to call you!" "You did a deliverance without my authority." "I couldn't get ahold of you. It couldn't wait."

"You went over my head. Please pack your things and get out. You're fired."

And in an instance, the promise of a ministry and a future were gone. I had never felt more demoralized and like more of a failure in my life. Line one of ministry resume: Fired after four months.

I was sure God was through with me.

12 DISAPPOINTMENT: PART TWO

"Preacher for hire. No credentials, one year Bible School graduate/dropout. Fired from first ministry job after three months. Will work for food."

It was about two weeks before Christmas, and my whole world fell apart. I packed my stuff at Youth Defenders, said goodbye to everyone, and moved out. I felt like an utter failure and was questioning whether I was ever even called. Why would I be fired by the same people that commissioned me for ministry? Maybe it was their weird way of sending people forth to preach…

I was so crushed. I reluctantly moved back into my parents' home – who were *so* hoping this last move would stick – and just sank into a deep depression.

But I had one more thing I'd promised to do before I faded away out of ministry hopes and dreams. I had to get Bozcat home.

Bozcat was a genuine hippie van. He belonged to a genius Bohemian musician friend I had met at Bible School, Jenney Evans. School misfits, we gravitated to each other and a few more kids that didn't quite fit the mold, and we formed the Crazy for Jesus Band.

We had one performance the day before I left for home. We did a song Jenney wrote called "Why No Revival?", which was based on a little booklet that addressed selfishness and hypocrisy in the church.

The school president, Sister Lindsay, was infuriated, to say the least, not understanding the context. She turned

69

to John Garlock, the school administrator (and my writing teacher and later lifelong mentor), and said, "I *never* want to see them on this stage again!" Dr. Garlock and I kept in touch for the rest of his life. Talking with him about that event years later (he remembered our performance very well) he said, "I thought you all were pretty good…"

That was January, and I moved back home to California. That August, before my new ministry job began at Youth Defenders, Jenney and a bandmate drove Bozcat from Dallas to California. They did two concerts at my home church in Topanga Canyon. I had planned on hitching a ride back to Dallas to see my Bible School friends and then fly home before I moved into Youth Defenders.

The van broke down two hours outside of L.A. A friend picked us up. We had the van towed to a repair shop and flew to Dallas to continue our journey. Jenney was going to send me money to replace the engine, and I would drive it back to Dallas later that year.

Now, in January, having been dismissed from my first ministry job, I could.

The last, futile act of a failed minister…

Oh, everything feels fatal when we're young, doesn't it?

So, in mid-January, I got Bozcat out of the shop, packed up, and hit the road. It was a long drive from L.A. to Dallas. I loaded up on junk food and coffee and made the long drive through Palm Springs and Phoenix. I would try to make it to El Paso and stay the night with one of my roommates from Bible School.

But, somewhere up a steep grade outside of Phoenix, the clutch gave out. Things were looking grimmer by the moment. I pulled into a rest stop, asked God for help, and what I can only describe as divine intervention given my total lack of car skills, I figured out that you *can* drive a manual transmission without a clutch! It took some timing, a little grinding of gears, but somehow I was able to get it going. I drove from Phoenix to El Paso with no clutch and a lot of prayer.

I called my friend Dan that evening. His mom said he was on a mission trip but would be back at 3 in the morning, and they would be happy to have me spend the night. I ate at my first El Paso restaurant before I went to their house, my first multicultural exposure to the world outside California. It was a Chinese American Mexican Buffet. I confess it was tastebud confusing but pretty great.

Dan got back in the morning after I had settled in and been sleeping a few hours. It was great to see each other. He would help me get the van fixed in the morning, then maybe follow me to Dallas the next day.

After a few good hours of sleep, Dan and I headed to the repair shop and dropped it off. I didn't want to tell him I had less than $100. In fact, as I recall, it was right about $38.00. I was counting on that for gas to get to Dallas.

"Hey, my church elders are meeting with a bunch of pastors at Wyatt's cafeteria across the street. We should go.

Maybe you could tell them a little about your vision for ministry." I could do that, but my "vision" was not fully formed. I wanted to give my testimony. I had a broken heart for broken people and a lost generation of fatherless kids.

We went to the luncheon, and after about 40 minutes of eating and pastor talk, they asked me to share. I just shared from my heart. Well, now we can go, right? "When can you come back?" What? They must have seen my puzzled expression. They discussed some possibilities among themselves, then said, "Can you come back and speak at a few of our churches and youth groups and maybe speak at the Crisis Hotline center? When could you come back? I was stunned. "I can be here next week," I offered.

We picked up the car. It was $37.50. The cloud was moving. I wanted to laugh and cry for joy at the same time!

I made a call to an old High School friend who would come and share the ministry time with me. I completed the return of Bozcat, and after a few days' visit with Bible school friends, I returned to El Paso.

That Sunday, I found myself standing in front of close to 1000 people sharing about the goodness and redemptive power of Jesus' love.

In one moment, the Lord took me from dislodged, purposeless, and disappointed, to stepping into the very place God had ordained for me to be.

God gave Joseph great dreams of his place in His plans when he was a boy. But from the vision to the fulfillment would take Joseph down many painful, lonely, and disappointing roads. Instead of being respected, he was hated by his brothers. Instead of being given a God-ordained place over others, he was sent to jail to be humiliated, betrayed, and forgotten.

Except by God. God had already known the steps Joseph would have to take to deal with his heart and all the things that could ruin his calling. And although it was painful, so much so that they literally laid iron into his soul, (Psalm 105:18) he stayed faithful in the disappointment, finally yielding it all to the God who loved him most. He surrendered. And in one moment, he went from prison to position, from humiliation to honor, from dungeon to destiny.

Disappointment – His appointment. He knows the way that we should take.

As I stood before the audience of nearly 1000, I asked God to forgive me for almost letting my disappointment in the way things had turned out to turning away from the call. Every disappointment was just a stepping stone that had led me here. I was determined never to doubt His ways again.

Disappointment -- His Appointment"

Change one letter, then I see

That the thwarting of my purpose

Is God's better choice for me.

- Edith Lillian Young –

-

An addendum to this little story: almost a year after my departure from the Youth Defenders, when I was going full force in ministry, Rev. Irene called me and asked me if I would help her set up a crusade in Florida. I gladly agreed. "I want you to know," she said, "I did not quite understand the need to let you go when I did.It was hard. I only knew it was God. Now I understand. Look at where you are now." I understood now, too. God "kicked me out of the nest" to get me to my next mission. He is faithful in it all!

13 KFC, A BIRD, A REDHEAD, AND A TRANSISTOR

It's so easy – too easy – to let life wear you out, make you cautious, make you wary, even cynical, even in ministry. It's hard to admit that, after years of unrelenting ministry, I had grown, what? Not callous exactly, but a combination of numb, weary, burned out, and empty.

And that's where this little story begins.

It was a typical winter day in the southwest, cool but not cold, sunny and snowless, and the envy of snowbirds and freezing Northerners everywhere.

I had set out on a fairly typical afternoon route doing errands – post office, bank, store, walk, home.

I was not having a good day. I felt talked out, stressed out, given out, and put out. Not fit for human interaction.

So I dashed out to run errands, hoping to minimize interaction and get away with a fakey plastered-on Christian smile that covered up my surly attitude pretty well. It worked on most days.

Not this day.

I rushed through the drug store and almost ran back to my car, having seen a flash of a thin young woman making her way across the parking lot. She was making her way toward me. Wants money, probably for drugs, I quickly judged. I gave at the office. Hurry…get in the car, and go…

But I wasn't fast enough, and I'd left my window down. Perfect timing. I started the car, she was right there, but I beat her to the punch. "SorryIdon'thaveanymoney," I rushed through before she said a word. "Oh, OK," she said sadly as I drove off and left her standing there.

Look, I don't blame you for judging me. It was callous, premeditated rejection meant to ensure my hasty exit and home to my safe little world where I could shut out the world for a while.

I got one block away, and Jesus smote my heart, and I wept. "Oh, Jesus, forgive me, please forgive me, what's the matter with me?" I rushed off to the nearest fast food place, picked up some KFC and a drink, and headed back, praying and asking Jesus to give me another chance.

She was not there. Anywhere. My heart was crushed. I had failed Jesus. I had a chance to show someone His loving face, and instead, I had driven off in a selfish huff.

I turned around in the parking lot to go home, and there she was – just a few yards away. "Excuse me!" I yelled, trying not to startle her. She turned around and came up to my car. "Here," I said, handing her the food. "I'm so sorry about before." She just smiled as she took the food. "What's your name?" I asked. "Missy, " she said, and I could see that almost all her teeth were gone. "Missy, Jesus loves you. And I will be praying for you," I said. She grinned brightly and broadly. "Thank you," she said quietly.

I wasn't any hero at that moment. I was a forgiven, wretched sinner that had forgotten where I came from. I was grateful God opened my heart and my eyes that day. I never wanted to forget the pit that He had dug me out of.

A few weeks later, I drove to California to end my year in my hometown, seeing my old high school friends and trying to rest and recoup for the new year. I was approaching burnout and asking Jesus to renew my heart.

I drove to Santa Monica, parked, and spent the afternoon walking up and down the pier, taking in all the interesting vendors, artists, dancers, singers, and even psychics and prognosticators. You could find almost all of lost humanity out here. I took in the salty Pacific air and the cool, cloudly breeze, stopping to watch the pelicans diving for fish and exchanging small talk with seagulls that were larger than chihuahuas.

I went to the pier's end, sat outside at a familiar Mexican restaurant, and ordered. I was drinking an iced tea and drifting into relaxation when I saw him. At the end of the pier was a red-haired man of indefinable age, somewhere between twenty and fifty years old. He was standing there alone, his hands all in motion. He was deaf. And I knew sign language. I was stunned as I watched him signing to the sky, to no one, to someone. "I miss you so much! Where are you? I love you. I miss you!" My heart just shattered, realizing the awful reality of what I saw – a man completely alone, homeless, friendless, begging the sky, or someone who had died, to respond.

Tears stung my eyes. "Oh Jesus," I prayed, "He's so alone! Please help him!"

At that moment – and I am not kidding – a one-legged seagull jumped onto the end of my plate and just stared at me. I just broke down. "You can have my food!" I said to him. He fearlessly pecked at my lunch. I paid the bill and left, hoping to find the man I'd seen. He was gone.

But halfway down the pier, I saw a homeless man, just standing there, eyes old and tired and hardly aware he was there. Beside him was a paper cup for donations and a handmade sign that said, "Please help me, I am playing music for you." I was undone. A life of a man of perhaps 70-75, reduced to turning on a transistor radio for spare change. I went right up to him. "What's your name?" I said, tears still coming down my face. "Tom," he said quietly, a bit startled. "Tom, can I pray for you?" "OK," he said. Unaware of a small crowd that had gathered, I lay one hand on Tom's chest and one on his head and prayed down heaven. I prayed for salvation, I prayed for blessing, I prayed for healing, I prayed that the end of his life would be a good, godly end and that he would be loved and taken care of. There were tears in his eyes when I was done. "Thank you," he said. God bless you's were exchanged. "I won't forget you," I said. And I haven't.

A homeless girl, a red-haired orphan, a seagull, and a transistor radio DJ – God used these loved bits of God's heart to challenge me, break me and remind me of what the Gospel is all about. "For God so loved the WORLD."

We get so caught up in our own worlds, and as believers, we get caught up in activities, social things, church picnics, and church committees that we forget there is a miserable, dying world out there waiting for kindness and salvation to come to their door. How will they hear without a preacher? Paul asked. And in case you didn't get the inference, that's you. That's me. We're the preachers. We are the bearers of good news.

But if we become hardened, if we ignore the human wreckage around us every day, how will they know?

Maybe you are shy and don't know how to start. I offer you a simple step. When you are in the store or restaurant, just ask the person serving you, "Can I pray for you for anything?" You might think you would be setting yourself up for rejection, but you will be shocked by how many people will say yes and open up their hearts to you. It could be the open door to lead someone to Jesus. You have to just be bold enough to ask the question.

People are hurting. The world is broken and lost. The opportunities are out there every day, perhaps with a homeless person, a grieving orphan, or even a transistor DJ.

Listen. Watch. Open your heart. We are His hands, His heart. Go into all the world. And watch Jesus change lives as you pray.

14 A VISIT ONE WINTER

One of the fun things about finding out I have a Jewish lineage is that I get twice the holidays that Christians get.

I'm not "devout" and don't call myself a "Messianic Jew," and although my cousin (who was married at the Wailing Wall) has yet to provide copies of our family proof of Jewishness (without which she couldn't have gotten married there) I just folded myself into the festivals, culture, and history and it's enriched and strengthened my walk with Jesus, I'm not a "Hebrew Roots" guy. They brought too much baggage to an already touchy area. It just made sense to me to learn all I that could about God the Son, who placed Himself into a Jewish body, a Jewish family, and a Jewish culture. So much of what Jesus said makes more sense to me now that didn't before. Seeing how Jesus was the perfect fulfillment of all of the commanded feasts of Israel was astonishing, and I enjoyed celebrating traditional Passover meals as well as many aspects of Rosh Hoshana and Yom Kippur that spoke so much to my heart of my need for ongoing repentance and awaiting Jesus' return.

I suppose there was something in me that just kind of knew ever since I was a young teen. I got saved at 15, and a year later, I got kidnapped by a group of kids who held a bible study at Chatsworth High School every lunch and insisted I be part of it. One of the first kids I met was a skinny 14-year-old kid named Gene. "Can you go to church with me?" he asked, and that's how I ended up going to Chatsworth Foursquare Church, where I stayed for three years and have some of my most fond memories in my early faith: Hearing the new Christian Rock group Love Song playing in the church parking lot, overwhelmed by the presence of God and the power of His love through this band; going to the altar in prayer during an 'afterglow" service, sitting sad and broken on the floor, and having Carl Burns, the pastor, sit next to me, put his arm around me and weep as he asked Jesus to touch and heal my heart; meeting Alice, a widow, who nearly every week gave me a little bit of money as a "donation" for my ministry, which I had not even begun yet but she knew would come; practicing with our little band "Isaias" every week at the Bread Box, our little youth building right behind the church. They were such powerful moments that helped form and strengthen me for the days ahead.

My friend Gene was actually born Jewish, raised Mormon, got saved, Spirit-filled, and was one of my best friends. I didn't hesitate when he asked me to go with his family to a Hannukah service at the Synagogue. And I suppose only after I learned about my Jewish lineage did I understand why I felt so absolutely at home at my friend's Synagogue.

Or why I felt even more at home at his wedding. Gene had actually backslid, come back to Jesus, and went on a missions trip to Cyprus with YWAM, where he met his wife-to-be from Switzerland. He asked me to sing at his wedding. It was a half Jewish half Christian wedding, and I sang Lamb's *Song of Ruth*. It was a beautiful wedding, and I did my best to honor God in my singing. I guess I did ok; Gene's great aunt came up to me during the reception, shook my hand, and said, "That was SUCH a LOVELY SONG! Are you married?" Yes, I felt more than at home. I felt like I was with family, family who needed to know the Messiah, the Hope of all Israel and the world.

Some of my Christian friends were not as thrilled about my newfound Jewish discoveries. I was totally shocked when two friends – separately – greeted my news of discovering that I was Jewish – by telling me Holocaust jokes. I'm not kidding. Antisemitism is alive and well, even in the church.

Giving up pork wasn't a religious decision for me. It's just that, coincidentally, months before I discovered my Jewish ancestry, eating pork started making me seriously sick. I stopped eating pork, I stopped getting sick. It was a health issue for me.

But for Christians, it was like telling them I don't want to take communion anymore. I wish I'd taken pictures of the shock on their faces. "Ham sandwich?" "No, thanks." "Not hungry?" "I don't eat pork." Slow pause. Mouth drops open. "WHAT?! Why not?!?" "Because it makes me sick," was the easiest answer. But it made me realize the church has a serious addiction to pork. Ham sandwiches. Ham salad. Bacon, sausages, all things pork. When a popular restaurant offered bacon shakes, that was about it for me.

I don't have a problem with other people eating it. I don't even mind having to bring my own food to church functions so I don't have to graze on grapes and chips and call it "all day dinner on the ground."

But I have to admit, I've had some fun with my non-Jewish church friends. "Isn't it weird," I said to my pastor one Easter, "How we celebrate Easter and the resurrection of our Jewish Messiah by going home and eating an unclean animal for lunch?" Just a thought...

There is a lot I understand that I didn't before by looking at the actual Jewish context of the Savior I love and serve. One of my favorite festivals is Channukah – the Festival of Lights. Unlike Passover, Shavuot, Yom Kippur, and Rosh Hashanah, which were commanded in the law, Channukah was the celebration of the miracle of the Menorah, when God miraculously provided oil to supply the Menorah for many days.

Although it wasn't an original festival, Jesus recognized it and celebrated it. Remember? "I am the light (Menorah) of the world." In fact, Jesus both represented and fulfilled every single feast God had ordained. I wish I had time to go into more details, but when you realize how perfectly God designed it all thousands of years before, it makes you stand in pure awe of His holiness and love.

Having said all of that, I confess that my understanding of all things Jewish leaves much to be desired. And all this background just to tell a very short story, but one that will stay with me for a lifetime.

It was a rather windy night, and it was one of the first days of Channukah. I had just picked up friends from Florida and had a nice dinner with them, returning just in time to light the candles.

Except, I couldn't remember which ones got lit that night. I told you I wasn't very good at this thing. My kitchen window was open a tiny bit, and I could hear the wind howling outside. I remember feeling safe and grateful for this night. But unable to figure out which candles were to be lit, I simply lit one and then called a friend who knew more than me. "I am not sure which candles to light tonight," I told them. "The first and second on the right," they replied. I'd gotten the first one right. As we talked, I watched the flame from the first candle expand and move from the first candle to the second by itself—no breeze, nothing – just a sovereign hand.

I lamely said, "You won't believe what happened. It looks like God saw my dilemma and lit the candle himself." It was more of a joke, in a moment of holy visitation, and when I got off the phone, I felt immediate grief and conviction. And I heard a gentle Voice, "How is it that you no longer recognize Me when I visit you?" I was crushed and in tears. "Dear Jesus, forgive me! Forgive me for not recognizing the holiness of this moment. O God, who am I, that you would visit me at all? Forgive me…" It was a moment of repentance and of the fear of the Lord.

How many times has the Lord come up next to us, looking for us to listen, to look, to recognize Him in the moment we are in? How many times has He longed for us to slow down, stop, look up, and realize He longs to fellowship with us, speak to us, heal us, challenge us, fill us with His grace and power and love?

Start by taking moments each day to open His Word and read, and asking, "Father, I am here. Walk with me in

Your Word. I want to know your heart. I want to understand your ways." Make it a daily longing and quest. And then carry that Word in your heart through the day and night, expecting the Light of the World to reveal Himself in every moment before you.

It is a sacred and holy thing to know that the God who created all, longs to stoop down and walk with His creation and call them His friend. Don't let even one opportunity to befriend Him pass you by!

15 NAVAJO

One of my favorite people was Rich Mullins, the popular 1980's Christian music artist that didn't really care for any of the trappings of major album sales or popularity. I loved that he moved to the Navajo nation, got a little trailer, and said he just wanted to teach little kids songs like Jesus Loves Me. His songs spoke deeply to my heart. His heart for the things of Jesus did, too.

I worked with a group called Mothers Against Sexual Abuse. Its founder, Claire Reeves, was one of the bravest people I knew in the fight against child abuse and an absolute Pitbull in the courtroom. I would have dreaded ever being on the other side of the issue from her.

"We've been invited to Four Corners, New Mexico to talk about sexual abuse issues. I'd like you to go if you can." Absolutely I would!

The night before I left, I learned that Rich Mullins had been killed in an auto accident. The irony wasn't lost on me that I was going into the Navajo reservation just after Rich left it and winged his way to heaven.

Two weeks later, I picked up Claire and her assistant, and we made the 3½ hour very dangerous drive from Albuquerque to Shiprock. That highway is like a trail of wreckage from all the drunk driving accidents they had on a continual basis.

We arrived safely in the early evening, and we met the therapist, who was our contact person for the week. A very nice lady, she was nonetheless thoroughly New Age.

"Hurry put these on. We have to go," she said after a quick introduction, handing us t-shirts and cutoff shorts. Claire and I looked at each other, confused. "We have to go in and join the elders for a sweat," the therapist said.

Oh, I hadn't planned on this! I was claustrophobic, heat-sensitive, subject to flashbacks, and allergic to burning things. But we had committed to this trip, so I changed, and prayed. A *lot*.

We entered the Hogan which had already been prepared for the evening. Claire, Charlotte, and I went in and took our places interspersed between the four elders of the Navajo nation – New Mexico, Arizona, Colorado, and Utah. After brief introductions, the Hogan was shut, and the ceremony began. I was praying fervently; I knew that the prayers in these settings were offered to their gods and ancestors. It was a totally pagan setting, one that was completely opposite of my faith in Jesus. In addition, it was a world God had delivered me from as a young man deeply entrenched in New Age and pagan practices. But I was here – and I knew God was up to something.

Sage and cedar were thrown onto the hot stone rock in the center of the Hogan. I was trying to breathe and trying not to panic. Navajo prayers were spoken. Then, one of the elders began to lead the discussion. "Now, we will talk about in which way our elders and parents dealt with sexual abuse." And I realized that this was a summit meeting. They discussed the lessons they had learned from their elders. We told what we had learned. Then the sage and cedar and prayers continued. I knew we were in dangerous territory spiritually, but God had brought me there. And I knew He would grant His protection from the demonic elements we were surrounded by. I prayed for a hedge of protection. I was there to pray to my God and to bring the Gospel of Jesus to the people.

We had a second and third round of discussions. It was insightful and heartbreaking. Sexual abuse was a huge problem among the People.

After the third session, Claire begged to be excused because of her heart issues and high blood pressure. It was against all protocol to break a sweat after it began, but they made an exception. As we went out and came back in, one of the elders came up to me and said, "Please hold this for me, brother," handing me the traditional peace pipe as he left to close the hogan. The significance of what he said was clear to me. I am not Native American. They rarely call *anyone* outside of their own "brother."

Then, I got it. This had been a test. "You want to talk to our people? You sweat with us first." The door was now wide open.

The week was not without battle. In fact, the tribe's local "skinwalker" (it's like our version of a devil worshipper or black magician) showed up at the meeting to discuss bringing us in a few weeks before and told them, "If you bring them in, I will make you all pay for it!"

Now, let me explain something. Skinwalkers bring terror into the native people. They are real, they are deadly, and they are evil. They have been known to transform into animals (don't dismiss that so quickly – I have seen similar things in the world of deliverance from demons), curse people, sleep in cemeteries. The threats weren't idle, and they were taken very seriously. But they took the risk.

I realized, after the sweat, that they had accepted us into their tribe for the time we were there. We had earned being heard.

That night we stayed at a house on the Colorado/New Mexico border that had been offered to us for the week. It was unnerving that a reservation patrol car sat up at the top of the road with his lights pointed at the house for hours. I finally went up and asked him what he wanted. "Everything ok?" he said. "Just checking." Friend or foe? I didn't know.

In the middle of the night, I was disturbed by the dishwasher going off. I wished the other people wouldn't decide 3 am was a good time to wash dishes!

The next day I asked my team about it. Neither of them had touched the dishwasher.

Well, having grown up in the world of shadows and spooky things, if this was all the skinwalker could conjure, I knew we'd be ok.

The next day, more than a hundred Navajo people gathered, mostly elderly, to hear us. There were greetings and an opening performance by the youth from the rehab center. They sang and drummed for several minutes, and what was I feeling? I felt their anger, immense sorrow, loss, emptiness, longing. Tears streamed down my face as I felt the pain of these lost youth.

During the break, I asked the rehab center's head counselor, "What is the abuse rate on the reservation?" "100%," she answered. I couldn't believe what I heard. Dear God, help us bring light and deliverance to these wounded people!

The therapist – who, bless her heart, was a dyed-in the-wool New Age follower who loved to talk about the rain gods and the stone gods and the ancestors, etc., etc. - had taken me aside before I was going to talk. "Whatever you do," she warned, "Do *not* talk about the skinwalkers, ok? Because it really scares people, especially the elders. So don't talk about them. Whatever you say, *don't* talk about the skinwalkers, ok?" "Ok," I answered. I got the impression she *really* did not want me to talk about the skinwalkers…

Claire spoke first. Then Charlotte. They were well-received. Then it was my turn.

"I want to talk about the skinwalkers," I said, and I saw the raw fear and concern on all the faces of the people there. And the not-very-happy face of the therapist.

"When I grew up, our tribes were different than yours. Nevertheless, we had our own version of skinwalkers. And they were evil, and they were destructive, and they destroyed lives, and they hurt little children. I was one of them. They were called devil worshippers. It is the same thing. And I was afraid of them too until, at the age of 15, Jesus Christ came and rescued me. And he set me free. And I have never feared them again, because Jesus has all power over all the power of darkness, including the skinwalkers."

Something broke. To a person, the entire audience got up on their feet and began to shout and applaud. I saw the fear leave their faces. I saw the enemy stand down! I shared the Gospel of Jesus who alone could set them free.

Immediately after my talk, the therapist and the Lakota chief took me to the back and began to smudge and sage me, scared for me. I appreciated their concern, but I also knew that the power of Jesus Christ would protect me from all harm, and I needed nothing else.

The rest of our time there was rich and rewarding, educational, and humbling, with many opportunities to tell people about Jesus. I knew I would carry the hearts of these people with me for the rest of my life. And we were honored by being presented with very personal gifts by all of the elders.

We were able to bring hope and healing, and most importantly, the love of Jesus, to this precious people that He gave His life for.

I think Rich would have been proud.

16 BLOCK WALLS

I learned something recently. There's a difference between block walls and rock walls. One, rock walls take more work and more skill, as you are cementing together various sizes and shapes of stones and rocks in some orderly, level, and hopefully, stable fashion. It seems to be one of the favorite building methods for backyards in the great southwest where I live. But they do tend to fall apart and develop cracks and holes after a while. And black widows love to live in those holes, so I am not a fan. I really, really hate spiders.

Block walls – cinder block walls – are usually rectangular and can be stacked and cemented rather easily. And they are also favorite hideouts for black widow spiders.

I used to be a spider killer, going out at night in stealth mode and stealth black clothes into my back yard, flashlight in my left hand, insect killer in the other. (No emails or letters from Peta lovers, please. Show me a picture of yourself petting a black widow spider, or rescuing a grateful brown recluse, or showing sad siders hiding in tiny rock crevices waiting to be adopted, and maybe I'll listen. No? Because they aren't cute and cuddly. So Kill 'em.)

I was sure that if my neighbors saw this, they would think I was nuts. That's ok. One summer, during a crazy monsoon and a violent downpour and lightning flashing every three seconds, I went to go upstairs and almost ran face-first into a huge black widow spider that had somehow sneaked in, threw a web from ledge to staircase, and waited…That was it for me. I killed them before they got in. It was them or me.

Cinder block walls can also get spiders hiding in them, but they are easier to spot, so I prefer them. At least I did until I had to work with them.

It was an unusually cold winter in Southern California, and it was an exceptionally rainy season. I was running, not so much from God, but from my own failures. Hiding like Adam, ashamed of my sins and trying desperately to find a safe place to heal. And I was running from the steps necessary to get healed – total surrender – brokenness – and letting God start again from the ruins of my life.

So like Jonah trying to do things my way rather than His, I ended up being part of a construction crew, a job I was not built or equipped for. But I woke up every morning at 4:30 am, piled in the truck with the crew, and we drove over to the construction site and worked hard until nearly dark, drove home, ate late, got three or four hours sleep, and started again the next day.

Our job took us to the little hilly suburban community just being built called "Lake Elsinore" (or El Snore as we lovingly called it.) We had been hired to build a gazebo and a block wall to go around the back yard. It was cold, and on the worst days, it was freezing rain and driving sleet.

The job was monstrously hard and reasonably simple. The foreman would meet us with a huge truck filled

94

with cinder blocks. We'd pick them up and walk them to the place where the wall was to be built. We would lay the bricks down straight and true: the first row, then cement, bring the next batch and put on the next row, straight and true, repeat until several rows of about 8 feet high and 50 feet long were raised up. Every muscle in my body was screaming by the third day, and I was desperate for God to talk to me. About anything.

We finished the job on Day Four and awaited the boss's inspection. He finally showed up late one morning, measured, wrote, remeasured.

"Tear it all down and do it again," he ordered. Our jaws dropped. "WHAT?!?" we collectively griped, "WHY?"

That was when the Holy Spirit moment came for me. I don't know if it happens this way for other people, but for me, in the course of an event or a conversation, I get a clear and undeniable knowing that I am about to hear something that is crucial to grasp and is eternal in nature – like being in a play and suddenly everything around me drops away, and the Spotlight shines and focuses on me, and God says, "Pay attention. This is very, very important." I know God is about to speak.

I was all ears at that moment as everything fell away but the words of the foreman, who spoke inescapable truth:

"The foundation is off 1/16th of an inch." He must have seen the, "So what?!" looks on our faces, so he continued with, "If the foundation is off even a fraction, it may look straight, but the whole wall will be unstable; it will get worse the higher you go. Eventually, it will all fall down. You have to make the foundation perfectly straight."

Suddenly all the missteps that had led me to this bleak hilltop, frozen limbs, aching muscles, bleary eyes moment made sense, as I realized there were foundation issues in my walk with Jesus. And He had allowed the wall to fall so we could go back to the beginning and make that foundation sure.

Thankfully, the true basic foundation of Jesus in my life was true. But the crooked bricks that came on top of that- unhealed hurts, bitterness, addictions, and fears – had skewed the wall until it was about ready to collapse under its own weaknesses. And it did. From that day, I surrendered, and God began to sort everything in the ruins out, clean the bricks up, and make sure my next row was built on the truth of the Word of God. He rebuilt me on a solid foundation of His love and grace. This time I was built to last.

Now, how about you? Did you begin well, but as you built your walk, did things start to show cracks, holes, maybe even nasty little destructive and poisoned spiritual spiders waiting to bite at every move? Did you start well and then end up with a building that was barely holding together, and you're wondering where you went wrong? It's ok. Sometimes God has to tear down faulty things in us in order to build eternal solid things. Sometimes the Potter has to break us and remake us on His wheel to make us into a thing of beauty and strength. Trust Him. He is true to rebuild us even out of the wreckage, from the wreckage.

And He is determined not to stop until we are conformed into the perfect image of His Son.

Father, we came to you damaged, and you graciously received us and caused us to be born again. But Lord, on Your sure foundation, we have built unsurely, often crookedly, hindered by sins and wounds that would have caused us to collapse unless you had stopped us and begun to take down and redo the wall of our walk. Oh, Jesus, it hurts! But we trust you. Rebuild us. Remake us. And don't stop until we have a walk that is unshakeable. Thank you. As CS Lewis wrote, "For this I bless you as the ruin falls; the pains You give me are more precious than all other gains." Amen.

17 BROTHER DAVID AND ME

I was just getting ready for Wednesday youth service when I saw a Facebook update from an old Bible school friend, Scott Hinkle, who has since school poured his life into street evangelism: "Our hearts feel a great loss of a great spiritual leader of our era, David Wilkerson…" "Oh, no!", I exclaimed. "No, no, no! Oh, dear Jesus, it can't be!"

I quickly confirmed that brother David had gone to be with Jesus just hours earlier.

I wasn't expecting the flood of emotions that overcame me. I had to hold back waves of tears so I could get through the youth service. I was thankful we had a guest speaker so that when I wasn't on stage, I was able to sneak into the back room to weep and to pray.

David is woven into the very fabric of my life and calling and has been since the very beginning when I came to Jesus.

I was fourteen when I read *The Cross and the Switchblade*, and it opened the door into Jesus' Kingdom for me. A sad, demonized, occult-bound alcoholic kid, I was at the end. I went on a trip with my parents. I took the book, which had been given to me by a persistent older gentleman named Ted Jantz that kept trying to drag me to this place called Action Life. I'd been once, and it had scared me to death. It was a house full of Christians singing and praying and talking about Jesus. Fallen so far into darkness that I had counted myself too evil for God to love, I didn't want to go back and be reminded what a worthless, hopeless loser I was.

But I did take the book Ted gave me. *The Cross and the Switchblade* was the story of a young preacher from Pennsylvania, David Wilkerson, who read in Life Magazine about young gang members in New York who were being tried for murder. His heart was broken, and he packed his car and headed off to go lead them to Jesus. Instead, he was arrested for storming into court with his Bible, trying to speak to the judge.

He didn't get to reach those kids. But David found killer Mau Mau gang leader Nicky Cruz, told him Jesus loved him and ended up getting beaten up for it.

As I read the story alone in my little motel room in Northern California – how Nicky Cruz had asked David what he thought now after he had beaten him up – and David's reply, "Nicky, you can cut me into a thousand pieces, and every piece will scream out, 'Jesus loves you!'" – my whole world was shaken. That one sentence cut through all the anger, fear, and doubt and exploded like a million bombs in my heart. I threw the book into the wall, screaming, "How come no one ever told me Jesus had that kind of power? How come no one ever told me He could love even the *worst*?"

Those simple words spoken through the broken heart and broken body of a man who left his comforts for the mean streets of New York were the words that led that broken little fourteen-year-old to cry out for help to whatever God was out there – and Jesus answered. Within a short time, I was His.

When David brought his crusade to Woodland Hills a year later, I went and heard him preach. I was riveted. I signed up for his monthly newsletters, which always included a teaching message. I was fed. I grew. Between his teaching, and later that of Rick Howard and John Garlock at Christ for the Nations, I felt God pouring into me, molding the character I would need for difficult ministry that was both uncompromised on truth and brokenhearted with God's love for the lost and the hurting. Each of these men was a cornerstone of that work of God in me.

I was already doing street evangelism and Bible studies in 1973, feeling the fire and stirrings of some kind of calling from God, but unsure of what to do with it.

"I had a vision," David's newsletter said that summer. There was an order form for a recording of the message God gave him about that vision. I ordered it, and when it arrived, I eagerly sat down to hear it. I was completely wrecked. For life. The power and anointing and truth of that message – and the urgency – were my call from God to lay everything down and surrender to the call to ministry on my life. I fell to my knees and wept and told Jesus, "Whatever it takes, Jesus, do it! Make me ready! I want to be one of Your last day servants!"

Do you think me foolish or naïve, these 38 years later, since we're "still here" and not raptured? I don't. That hour prepared me perfectly for this hour, the very hour we are in. It *is* the last days. I *am* one of those servants.

God heard my prayer the day I heard David's message, and six months later, God ordered me to Christ for the Nations. David's letters went with me. He spoke at CFNI, and God gave me a word for him, which I wrote out and delivered to his assistant. But who was I? Yet somehow I know he read it. I had no thought that our lives would ever intersect in any significant way.

I did know that he was getting mocked and battered for his vision. Come on – the Soviet Union collapsing? But I knew he'd heard God. Now nearly 90% of that vision has come to pass.

I left CFNI. My next warrior-coach didn't teach – he dragged me onto the streets and taught me how to be bold and fearless. Rev. Glenn Adkins put armor on me and kicked me into super-battle mode. (You need to read his book about his own remarkable calling, *Never A Dull Moment*, for a powerful testimony of street-level evangelism.)

When I started my own ministry, I wrote a little handwritten newsletter on the beach of South Lake Tahoe about my broken heart for lost youth and my longing to reach them for Jesus. Summer, 1976. Please, I told my handpicked 17 friends – can you pray for me, pray about supporting my ministry financially every month? A few did. Three friends STILL do!

I didn't send David that newsletter. But I did the next one, and the next…I sent them for four years, never knowing if he even read them. And I kept reading his.

"David Wilkerson's office calling for Greg Reid," the voice on the other end of the line said. What?! It was the spring of 1980. "This is he…" "Brother David is doing an evangelistic outreach in San Francisco this summer. He was wondering if you could come to visit with him and perhaps go with a team to do some teaching classes on evangelistic issues." I was stunned. It had been a time of great testing and great waiting that year – and the answer to many prayers was in that call. How did he know I was close enough to make the two-hour drive to Lindale from Arlington? Oh – he *was* reading my newsletters! "Yes, ma'am," I said, and we arranged my trip for two days following.

Listen, I'm not a man worshipper or a Christian celebrity groupie. I'd already met Pat Boone, a state senator, a magazine publisher, the president of the Assembly of God church, the president of the United States' mother and sister.

But concerning David Wilkerson, I was totally intimidated!. It wasn't so much him as the prophetic anointing he carried – severe, direct, and shocking in the Lord's ability to lay your heart bare in a moment. At least, that is what his preaching did to me.

So, I was very nervous about meeting him. Because although the Spirit had anointed my call, I was still pretty much a young goofball. You can see my concern.

The Lindale ranch was beautiful, like a new Jersualem – trees, lakes, cabins, offices.

Meeting David was as scary as I anticipated. He was no-nonsense and to the point. It was a mistake to crack jokes around him. I found that out the hard way.

We quickly got down to details, and I joined the team. He called his son Gary to settle me in for my overnight stay, show me the offices and property, and see that I got fed. Gary had a great, goofy sense of humor like mine, making me wonder about humor's genetic properties.

We met up with guys from the Dallas Holm Praise Band and ate and joked and played Uno till the wee hours.

I left with a large check from World Challenge to support my ministry – support that continued and sustained my work for another three years, every month. I was humbled – and deeply grateful.

San Francisco that summer was life-altering. I never did get to teach. But I was soaked in street evangelism for several days. People came to Christ – people rejected Christ – and I even got punched in the face by an angry gay man on Polk street.

But the moment I remember most was seeing David and his wife Gwen outside our coffee house in the Tenderloin, the most dangerous block in the city where people were being shot and stabbed every night just across the street – as this world respected and revered couple just stood and talked to and wept with and prayed for drunks and hookers and addicts and the homeless and the hopeless.

I said, "Jesus, I want to be like that." Just humble, real people doing real ministry.

My "fear" of David lessened, and my love for him and Gwen just grew. In an age when superstar Christians were driving Mercedes, dripping diamonds, and dropping like flies from infidelity, excess, and phoniness, I found my role model for living like Jesus, come success or failure.

And I was VERY aware that the very vision that God used to call me to ministry had cost David plenty. Only when I had written my own explosive and largely unwelcome book, *Trojan Church*, did I grasp what it might have been like for David to obey in the proclamation of truth, knowing it might be ministry suicide. I remember well the flood of ridicule and criticism leveled at David: Doomsday preacher. Sensationalist. Prophet of doom. It had to have hurt. But it changed him not one bit from his course, even when the formerly adoring Christian media distanced themselves. David just went on, seeking God's will and His Word.

Something of that was put in me, somehow, so that when ugly emails, harsh letters, loss of support, and a dearth of preaching invitations became a reality following my book's publication, I remembered people like David who had gone before, took the hits and kept going.

I could only say, "I could not *not* do it. I have to obey God as best I can," and keep on.

A year or two after San Francisco, David came to El Paso for a crusade. I'd called and asked to speak to him while he was here. I was hurting. I was burnt out. Despite the weariness that inevitably follows a night of preaching under the anointing, he told me to wait on his tour bus and he'd see me after the service.

I won't share all the details of our visit. I'll just say that three things stand out in my memory: One, he told me he had been to some of the darkest places on earth, and El Paso was the darkest he'd ever been to. And, "If I were you, I'd get out of this town and never look back." (I'm still here. It's even darker now. And the minute I'm decommissioned and reassigned, I will be shouting for joy.)

And I remember him speaking to me about struggles with sin and temptation. "Son, it's okay to struggle with sins on the periphery of your life," he said, illustrating the circle with his hands. "But if sin ever gets to be in the CENTER of your spirit, you are in real trouble." I never forgot that. I never will. I have taught it.

The third thing I remember is how this internationally known man of God set aside everything in a time of lateness and exhaustion to minister to an insecure, scared young preacher. If I was bleeding on the street, I am convinced the whole slate of Christian superstars would have passed on by. David was a Good Samaritan who stopped to bind me up. Rare, even now. Even today, it's limos and bodyguards and $200,000 a night preachers and flowers and fruit baskets in the contract.

How completely, disgustingly un-Jesus-like. And how glad I saw in David how it *should* be. I've sought to be like that ever since. My "contract" to speak is verbal; my requirements a hotel, transportation, love offering and a bottle of water when I preach. I pray that never changes.

Two years later, I was not in a good place, and rather than "deal," I denied. I wrote to David. He replied with a searching, 'too-many-questions to ask myself' letter.

And, I didn't want to, though I did eventually. But at the time, in a knee-jerk reaction, almost like a teen confronted by his dad, I wrote an angry reply. Oh, how I regret writing that letter! He never replied. I remember neither his letter nor mine today. I just know I had repaid his kindness and confidence by biting him. I have tears even now. I felt I'd let him down, and God especially. I figured David probably wrote me off.

Nevertheless, I still received his newsletters – and I still sent him mine, not knowing if he even read them anymore.

I returned to El Paso in 1987, and God opened up the most dangerous, explosive, and real mission I'd ever done. We weren't just on the mean streets. We were at the very gates of hell, snatching kids out of the pit of demonism, devil worship, sexual abuse, and worse. I knew this was it: this was the battle God had prepared me for. Every month, I documented every detail in my newsletters. David never responded.

There was one message from his secretary, saying David had a word for me and wanted me to call back. I did, but we were unable to connect. I will never know this side of eternity what it was, and I feel that loss. But today I realized, he'd been thinking of me; more, Jesus was, and said, "David, this is My Word concerning Greg Reid…"

I suppose, being the person that always feels like he's in trouble, part of me was afraid it was a *bad* word! But it could have just as easily been an encouraging one. I'll never know, But my heart warmed today as I realized, I know he took that word, and prayed for me.

David's son in law contacted me two years later and said his father in law, David, told him to call me when they moved here to do homeless ministry. We met for lunch, and I brought my co-ministry partner Tim. It was apparently not for me, but for Tim to help them in their mission. It was a disappointment, but in retrospect, God was moving Tim and I in different directions, and though I was saddened by the lost opportunity to reconnect with the World Challenge ministry and the Wilkersons, I knew I was following Jesus in a different direction. Still…

…the other day as I was in my garden, thinking about the falling out I had with David, I asked God, "Did he lose confidence in me, Father? Did he?" and almost immediately I heard the Lord say, "He told his son in law to call you when he came to El Paso. He did not lose confidence in you." I thanked God for that kindness that comforted my heart in my own private loss.

The years have passed. I've played "The Vision" for three generations of kids now, all challenged and stirred by it.

My salvation, which came through the Cross and the Switchblade, was written about in my book, *Nobody's Angel*, and spoken in every testimony I have given to crowds of teens across the country.

Every month, faithfully, newsletters came from World Challenge with written sermons from David. The years went by...I sent him *Nobody's Angel*...and lastly, *Trojan Church*. I never knew if he read them, but I thanked him when I signed them for his obedience to the Lord that had so touched my life.

I knew he was approaching 80. Walking through so many losses of friends and family and spiritual parents and mentors in the last 15 years, every time I received a letter, I thought, "Is this it? Is this the last one?" I saw some of his preaching on the internet. I wept with conviction as I saw them, and I showed them to our youth at our High School bible study at my home. It was the same man – the same anointing – the same conviction – the same uncompromised Word of God filled with broken compassion. Like Daniel – steady through the decades, unimpressed by baubles, one foot on earth, and the other already in heaven. Maybe more.

As I struggled through youth that night when I heard David died, I learned he had not gone quietly into that good night but was killed in a car wreck. Just like him, I thought. He did nothing expected. And what little I did know of him, going quietly was not him. He was ministry and fire and Gospel to the bone. And to the end.

The Bible says to give honor to whom honor is due, and he was due that. He was very human, flawed, and sometimes conflicted. But his heart and ministry was written large on my life, in a way he did not know, and had he, he would have probably just roughly said, "Give the glory to God, son, not to me!"

And I am. Because I really do know, it was *Jesus* who spoke through David to Nicky Cruz, and then to me. It was *Jesus* who gave David the vision that burned my life up for the ministry. It was *Jesus* who nudged David to invite me to San Francisco, to support a struggling ministry for three years, to speak through David to me in an hour of great struggle. I honor the obedience of His servant David. He was, in my estimation, the last of two of the Lord's giants, though he would no doubt cringe at even that statement.

But I have had many years to survey the land here and afar, and the fact is, we are in some of the very bleak days God showed David in his vision. And I may live to see the end of it. There is a famine for the Word of God in the land, and little real vision and the caliber of most ministers and ministries is as weak and unanointed and powerless as I've seen in my life. There is so little anointed preaching or conviction or standing on the integrity and truth of God's Word. My heart has cried and longed for God to raise up prophets among the youth in this hour – and that I could possibly be used to help raise them up.

When David departed, in the Spirit it was like the sound of the felling of a giant Redwood tree, followed by an aching, awful silence and a void. I believe he was one of the last true prophets of our time.

I know where he is. And where we are. And I have been crying out to God, "Lord, raise up a generation of prophets in his stead to scare Satan right out of this generation!" It will take that caliber of young people to bring real conviction and break through the hardened hearts and broken lives of this generation. A generation of Word-soaked, prayer-bathed, unafraid proclaimers of truth and God's love like David was. Like I've prayed to be.

At David's memorial, they spoke of the necessity of passing the torch – but passing it LIT – and David surely did that.

I know I was just one of the thousands of lives he touched. You know, there was a story told and retold until people were sick of hearing it – about a boy throwing dying starfish back into the sea as they washed up by the thousands, and a man asked the boy if it really made any difference. The boy picked up one starfish and said, "It does to this one."

Well, I'm the starfish. And God used David to throw me into Jesus' sea of life. Beyond allegory, I was a shattered life that first heard that God could love someone as hopeless as me from David's book – and heard the call to ministry through his vision – and was lifted to service through his invitation – counseled through his care, supported through his ministry and emboldened through his message. I thank You, Jesus, for using that flawed, anointed vessel to write Your Word and vision for my life in large letters on my heart. By Your grace, Jesus, I will pour out all that was poured into me for Your Kingdom. In this hour, may You raise up all those who have not bowed the knee to Baal. Fill the station vacated by our brother with thousands just as committed, just as real, and just as anointed. May I be counted among them.

18 ALREADY RODE

I have always loved youth ministry. Ever since I was a youth myself, I've been 100% invested, heart, mind and soul in youth outreach. I felt beyond blessed beyond words to be able to be part of the growth of young lives into adulthood and the Kingdom of God.

I didn't do it all for Jesus. I did it for me, too. Up until 15, what bright spots of my life I was given were blighted by the ugly hand of darkness and abuse. Then my remaining adolescence was spent in repair – painful, grueling healing that came one tiny step at a time.

Nevertheless, youth ministry came naturally to me. In my twenties and thirties, I experienced a bit of re-do of things I missed – that even though I experienced some of the things as a boy, it was always clouded by wounds I couldn't seem to overcome.

So when I became fully engaged in youth work in my thirties, it was more fun than I'd ever had. Frankly, it was a miracle.

I was living in Everman, Texas, when I was 31, and I found myself surrounded by a handful of neighborhood kids who were curious about God, naïve about the ways of the world, and wanting to know who Jesus was. We spent long hours talking, having Bible studies, and just having fun.

And did we have fun! Bike riding, Dictionary, foosball…and "the" waterpark. The Dallas/Ft Worth Metroplex had one of the largest, coolest waterparks anywhere. And my best memories were of taking our little gang there and just hanging out from morning to sunset.

I moved away, and I was given another youth group – a little rougher – well, a lot rougher! No waterpark, but rock climbing in the desert, football, basketball and iceball fights in winter. I got a few injuries in the fun, all of them were worth it. Most notably, the "ice ball" fight on the mountain that hit me square in the head and sent me falling backward (unharmed) but also resulted in ripped jeans and a prickly pear cactus that had attached itself like a tail to me in the fall. Which those charming kids didn't tell me about until an hour or so later, which explained their unexplained pointing and snickering…

I was continually thankful to be both buddy and mentor to a great bunch of kids. And always, forever, they are in my heart.

The next few years following the closing of that beautiful work of God – which included marriages, two funerals, and some kids going into ministry – were personally painful and difficult. Both my mother and father died, two years apart. And although I still did out of town youth ministry, at home, I was simply trying to grieve and recover.

Then, a new door opened. A youth outreach opened up right across from the youth center we once ran. I suddenly found myself once more immersed in youth work – praying, playing, hiking, discipling, pouring out. It led to a small church, a small youth group, volunteering, and then youth pastoring for seven years.

Although I was older than the conventional youth pastor, I jumped in with all fours and gave it my all. My energy was undiminished, my enthusiasm strong.

It was during one of the last years that I felt the change. As young Jesus-disciples grew, I watched them start to take on younger kids to teach, encourage, and pray for. There was a natural "letting go," realizing I had to now allow my spiritual kids to take it to the next generation.

Then the church began to change direction. It was trying to grow. There was a new emphasis on numbers, but more – there was a subtle shift toward a younger demographic, and a more fun youth group.

Some questioned whether I was still up to the job at my age.

That hurt, I admit. I had become a bit of a grizzled old lion, but I wasn't a dinosaur. It wasn't about age for me: It was about pouring out my life to raise up a new generation of young lions to bring Jesus to their friends.

I knew my days were numbered after that, so I did my best to give it my all on the way out.

My last mission trip with our kids was painful, wonderful, eternal, and Spirit-filled. I baptized several in our hotel pool. We laughed and cried, knowing the inevitable was coming.

God in His wonderful grace allowed us to go the very same waterpark I had gone to decades before, with other youth, each of them still remembered and loved. It was kind of a last hurrah, and I felt it. So I was determined to enjoy every moment, ride all the slides, revel in the moments.

As we approached my favorite slide, I was with two of our guys, and I was looking forward to riding this three-rider raft with them.

But when we got to the front, we were separated. They put my two kids in with a third person, and I was left to wait for the next raft. The park attendants took two others, and my two, and they were off, and I suddenly felt lost, alone, sad, lonely, and hurt.

Oh, I know, I'm an adult, and you may not ever feel little kid feelings. But I did, and it took my breath away, and tears came to my eyes because (and I can always tell when it's happening) I was in the grip of an important Jesus-moment. "Not fair," I said under my breath. "I was really looking forward to that ride with them, Jesus."

The words were clear, unmistakable:

"You already rode."

Suddenly I saw a far-reaching crystal-clear landscape of my years in youth ministry.

I had my turn. I rode the exhilarating rides and the adrenaline-fueled adventures for years. Now it was *their* turn, to grow up, to have the once-only adventures ahead of them, to do for others what I'd been allowed to do for and with them — and it was mine to let go. It was a holy- and terribly painful — moment of surrender. "Into Your hands, Jesus," I whispered.

The inevitable came, swift, painful (as church changes often are), and irreversible. I was neither fired nor let go – simply put into impossible situations so that I pulled the plug myself – as I reluctantly did – to avoid a greater shredding of the youth group away from the larger church. It was the hardest thing I ever did, or may ever do. Youth ministry was my heart, and it ripped my heart out to let go.

I trusted God for what was ahead…and jumped.

Gratefully, youth ministry continued in another place, in another setting. I once again learned that God is at work in all things to produce good. And that what the enemy wants to intend for evil, God turns for good. Always.

I learned that there comes a time to let go and bow out, not stand and fight.

I take encouragement from the story of David's mighty men told in 2 Samuel 21:15-17.

"When the Philistines were at war again with Israel, David and his servants with him went down and fought against the Philistines; and David grew faint. Then Ishbi-Benob, who was one of the sons of the giant, the weight of whose bronze spear was three hundred shekels, who was bearing a new sword, thought he could kill David. But Abishai, the son of Zeruiah came to his aid, and struck the Philistine and killed him. Then the men of David swore to him, saying, "You shall go out no more with us to battle, lest you quench the lamp of Israel."

David was a fierce warrior. Though just a boy, and only a shepherd, he had the heart of a shepherd, he had the heart of a warrior that took him from tending sheep to the front lines of the war against Goliath. And he won and became a warrior, then a King. Armies and kings trembled when they heard David and his army were on the move.

But as the years progressed, David's eagerness to fight was beginning to be met with concern by David's closest men. Finally, they pulled him back. "And David waxed faint…then the men of David swore to him, saying, 'You shall go no more out with us to battle, that you don't extinguish the light of Israel." (2 Samuel 15b-17b)

As I read this, I understood the pain David must have felt that he had to come off of the front lines as battle commander and first soldier. I am a spiritual soldier, and the frontline is in my blood.

But, "You already rode." I did what I did, and I'd moved from a young youth evangelist/pastor, almost "one of them," to a place where God was saying, "You've fought alongside them, as one of them. Now, father them, lead them and teach them how to fight the battle."

The transition was painful and jarring when it happened, but I trusted it was a withdrawal from the front of the battle, not a retirement from the war. And so it was and is, and I am grateful. If I learned anything from the great General George Patton, it was that the frontlines didn't kill him, but the prospect of civilian life long before a car accident took his life. He was a warrior at heart. Though not on the "frontlines" of youth ministry like I was, God has allowed me to remain a warrior in this generation, for this generation.

Are you being transitioned? Has God brought you to a place where He is saying, "You already rode; it's time to let another take the reins"? God knows your fear, your uncertainty, perhaps your hurt at a painful church dealing, firing, or unexpected move from a loved ministry, place, or location. "You already rode." "Yes, Father, I trust You." Let that be your humble prayer. God is not through with you! Remember that Daniel was not just a voice to a generation, but to all generations until the end of his life, and now beyond. For those that love and serve Him, there is always "God's next" until He calls us Home.

Not decommissioned – recommissioned! Wait for it! He has yet need for all your gifts and experience, and it will be better than anything dreamed of. Not retired but repositioned! Not discarded nor replaced in His House, but refit, retooled and re-armored.

God always has His Next. Let the others do what you did, and encourage and pray for them, parent them, and put your hand to the plow of God's Next! Truly, the best is still ahead!

19 FATHER

I have always loved my father. My fondest memories of him were when I fell asleep in the car on the way home as a little boy, and Pop would pick me up and carry me into the house and tuck me into bed. I loved the soft snuggle into his neck that always smelled of Old Spice. There was no safer place in the world than my father's arms.

He also sang to me when I was little. There was an old Doris Day song he would sing: "I love you, a bushel and a peck, a bushel and a peck and a hug around the neck." That's how I got my father's nickname: Gregory Peck. I would give anything to hear him sing that song to me again.

I don't know exactly what happened. But some time when I was around eight or nine, Pop stepped away from me. No more hugs. No more songs. Just distance, and an undefined anger. Pop was unhappy. He and mom were fighting.

Unfortunately, I overheard one fight from my room. All I could hear was Pop yelling, "You're always coddling him!" And Mom: "You never loved him!"

I can't say to this day with 100% certainty that it was about me, but my whole world came apart right then.

Mom came down to my room after. "Are you and Pop going to get a divorce?" I asked in a trembling little boy voice. "I don't know," she said, throwing me into limbo, fear, freefall.

Pop lost his job. He nearly died from an asthma attack, then nearly died from a fall down the stairs. He was disappearing from us. Then our house burned down, and Mom and Pop went into 100% survival mode. They were trying to save their marriage. They were trying to rebuild their lives. They were hoping for the best for their three boys, that somehow, they would survive too, unable to fully protect us from the onslaught of adolescence.

Did they love us? Oh, yes, they did. More than the whole world.

But neither of them had good parents. Pop had two alcoholic, violent parents. His mother died, his father married his mother's sister, and soon Pop was kicked out and living out in the streets as a young teen, sleeping under porches and eating out of garbage cans.

Mom's parents were violent drunks, too. She and her brother were offloaded to my grandmother's sister when they were tiny children. The void it left in my mother's heart was for a lifetime. And even though she managed to maintain contact with both parents after the war, "so the boys can know their grandparents," she never got over the rejection. Pop said when grandma died, mom just sobbed and said, "All I ever wanted was for her to tell me once that she loved me!"

Why am I including this? Because in retrospect, I am astonished that, not ever knowing the love of a mom or dad, they loved us so well – not in outward affection, how could they do what was never done for them? – but in caring for us, instructing us, teaching us. And they were always there in presence, if not in demonstrations of affection.

We were not a Christian home. And as with all nonchristian homes, the devil had a field day with all of us. My brothers and I were adrift. I fell into a pit of darkness and despair only God could deliver me out of. And He mercifully did.

But the wounds were so, so deep. Like many kids in our generation, especially sons, the "dad need" was a gaping wound. Without a safety net, I wrecked my life. And I knew I was responsible for that wreck, not my father.

After I received Jesus, I worked hard to bridge that gap between my Pop and I. Once I stopped using every conversation with them as a sermon, I realized only Jesus could save my mom and Pop. (He did – years later.)

So I just tried to be the best example I could be of what a Christian was, and I prayed, and loved him.

Changes came. He softened.

In my 21st year, Mom was out of town. My brothers were gone. Pop and me...alone for the first time since I was little.

So, we had Taco Bell for dinner. I know he was as nervous as I was. We were almost strangers. All he probably carried with him was memories of carrying his little boy home on his shoulder from the car.

After some minimal talk, he talked:

"Son, I know I've been a terrible father. I just wanted you to know (it's not because I didn't love you, his hidden words said) it's because I never really had a father. My father was an alcoholic. I didn't know how to be a father. I'm sorry, son."

"It's OK, Pop, you've been a good dad. I love you." "Well no I haven't, but thank you son. I love you too."

It was a half minute major healing for both of us. He was free from the guilt. I was free from wondering if he loved me. Of course, he loved me! And our relationship would grow till the day he died. God is so good.

So why was I still bleeding out over the lost years?

There was an era in the modern church where all kinds of books were written about healing – physical, emotional, spiritual. The "inner healing" movement began, and I was diligently learning, weeding out the unscriptural elements, and incorporating the scriptural ones into my own walk and ministry.

Secretly, still wanting to heal the "dad wound," I still agonized over the "lost years" I could never regain.

I read one "inner healing" book that told of a man with a dad-wound whose counselor, through "prayer imagination," led him to go back in his mind to the ballgame his dad missed, and "imagine" Jesus appearing to play catch with him.

Look, I know the counselor was well-intentioned. And I have to ask advance forgiveness for telling you my reaction was, "that's the DUMBEST thing I've ever heard."

Because I know Jesus is not an imaginary friend. He is Lord and King.

And no matter how much I may have had Jesus show up in my imagination as a substitute dad, he wasn't my Pop. Those years were *lost*. I knew that, and yet I still agonized over that loss.

I was in ministry, so I had the perfect Brave Face to cover my pain.

But God wasn't through with the "dad-wound" thing. He wanted to heal me. I had finally decided to bury the wound, nothing can be done. But it was still affecting my life and relationships. I was emotionally needy and self-destructive, and I regularly nuked healthy relationships.

My heart was hardening...

And then, mercifully, one Sunday I was in church singing, heard the sermon, waited for the closing prayer.

The pastor stopped. "I feel like someone here is suffering so deeply over your relationship with your father. God wants to heal you."

My heart shattered. The person everyone in this 100+ church saw as calm, spiritual and in control, broke into a million pieces and wailed. And wailed. The shocked pastor could only dismiss church and wait until I was through.

But I left empty. If God wanted to heal me, I thought, it didn't happen.

That healing happened just a few months later. I was at my home church in California, and a friend had graciously lent me their apartment when they were out of town so I could pray and seek some healing.

I locked myself in about 7 that night. I lay down on the floor and prayed. I got down on my knees and prayed. All I could feel were the years lost with my Pop. I wept and wept. "Please, God, I NEED MY DAD!" It in fact, was more than a cry of an adult. It was the cry of a child. I cried until I was sore. But there was more.

The Lord's voice was clear and startling:

"Die to the need to have your father."

Of all the words I have ever had from God, this was the most absolutely devastating. I wanted kind words, I wanted to feel it was better, I wanted to be healed! But not this! The dam broke, and I sobbed until every muscle in my body hurt. "Allright! Allright! I surrender to my need to have my dad!" I screamed. "I can't have those years! It's not his fault! It just can't ever happen! Jesus, help me to die to the need for a dad! God, *be* my Father!" The tears seemed endless. Time was irrelevant. I lay on my back after many hours, exhausted, completely empty.

I saw Jesus on the cross. He was taking all my pain when He was crucified. *All* of it. He took my pain of all the lost years of a child. "I surrender, Jesus." And suddenly, I felt the exchange. His death for my sins and brokenness. And in receiving His perfect blood sacrifice, I could feel Life - Resurrection Life - and healing flood into that bottomless wound, that dad-wound, and filled it completely, utterly, forever. I got up from the floor healed.

"Jesus, I forgive my father. Lord, *You* are my father."

From that moment on, the hurts of those years were gone. Completely.

Jesus didn't change the reality of my past. He removed the sting of the loss.

Because of that healing, I was able to have 16 more wonderful, healing, revealing, eternal moments with my father before his passing. They were times without my own wounds robbing him and I of any more time, and time that would be a bridge leading Him to Jesus. I got better than getting the lost years back. I got new years untainted by sin and sorrow.

I have come to understand that God never made perfect parents. If He had, we might not turn to Him. All flesh fails – parents, children, friends, spouses.

Almost all of us carry a past relationship wound – an absent or abusive father or mother, a divorce, a death, a betrayal. And God heals each of us differently.

But in that moment, I came to understand: Jesus paid it all, and He became it all in that moment: "For he hath made him to be sin for us, who knew no sin; that we might be made the righteousness of God in him." (2 Cor. 5:21) The perfect exchange – His healing for our hurt.

What hurts your heart? Just know that even though you can't redo the past, you don't have to live with the pain of it. Jesus felt it all, died from it all, the sin, the brokenness, the suffering of lost, sinful humanity. And on the third day, He rose in resurrection life. And as we surrender and die to those things, in the Great Exchange, you too will be healed – life for death, healing for hurt, new life for old!

How good our Father is!

20 BETWEEN HEAVEN AND EARTH

CS Lewis said, "The fact that our heart yearns for something Earth can't supply is proof that Heaven must be our home."

There is a longing in our hearts for a home we cannot see, a place of belonging and beauty and sweetness that we cannot experience here on earth but merely catch glimpses of in this life. We have longings for things that nothing in this life can satisfy, telling us that we were made for another world, one that this world is a mere shabby shadow of.

We know this, don't we? Our hearts are filled with aches and desires and longings that nothing quite satisfies. We're like little kids that stay up all night in anticipation of a long-awaited trip to Disneyland, or for the excitement of Christmas presents, only to wake up the day after feeling empty, sad, and let down.

Life sometimes feels like a big Christmas letdown. Excited to graduate! The day after, letdown, and fear of what's next. On to college - excitement! New friends, new adventures, a career! Graduation - letdown, then on to the working world...

Everyone dreams of falling in love, their wedding night, kids, growing old together. And there is joy in all of these things, a temporary joy, but also a certain emptiness, as well, the sense that as wonderful as these things are, that's not *it*. The longing for something beyond us remains.

I first became aware of that longing through music. From an early age, I was drawn to music, but more – I was drawn to the sounds of the meadowlark near the lake, the waves crashing on the beach, the wind whistling through the pine and eucalyptus trees surrounding our house, the constant drip and then pounding of rain and then thunder and then receding rain on the roof. All these things spoke to me. They made me ache inside for something I did not understand. I collected music and played the piano from an early age, looking for a certain sound I couldn't define. I would just walk in the hills and sit by the creek and listen…feeling all achy and lost inside, because something in those things spoke to me and drew me into a world I could not see, because it was a Kingdom I had not yet found. It was a heaven I had not yet graduated to, and yet I felt the certainty that there was something – somewhere – where these inner longings would be fulfilled.

I would listen to particular songs, and particular portions of them like Beau Soir by Debussy over and over again because it took me outside of my own miserable life and loneliness and fears and let me get a glimpse into something greater than myself, and better and more infinitely more beautiful than anything this world had to give. But where was it?

I found my first answer the night I surrendered my heart to Jesus and I was born again. My dull, sin-stained ugly life was suddenly alive and vibrant with eternal life and everything was made new. The next day I looked out the window and saw color for the first time in my life.

As I got older, I began to understand these internal longings were graces from God, His calling and wooing, His turning our attention and our hearts to something only He could give.

Later, my spiritual mother - a wonderful little Baptist lady in her 80's who loved Jesus with all her heart – used to describe heaven, as the Bible told it, as she knew it would be. "Eye has not seen, ear has not heard, nor has it entered into the heart of man the things God has prepared for those who love Him," she would tell us with her far-away spiritual gaze like she was almost there. "Look around you," she said, pointing to the beautiful canyon, green trees and bright flowers that covered the hills we could see from her humble little home she had named, "The House of the Four Winds." "If this earth is this beautiful, and it is under a curse – can you imagine what it will be like when the curse is removed?" She put in our hearts a longing, not just for a Person – Jesus – who she said would *be* heaven – but for a Place we had not seen, but had tasted of in our walk here with Him. She made us long for that Home.

It was a beautiful day in the first part of May, and I was a young man just beginning my walk in ministry. I had moved to another town and grown close to a group of college-age and slightly older lovers of Jesus – young people who were on fire for God and couldn't get enough of Him, or each other. It was a deep and wonderful taste of real fellowship, not just see-you-and-say-hi at church once a week fellowship, but committed relationships where we were truly like family. We spent the morning at church, and then gathered at the park and spent all day together. We ate, we laughed, we prayed, we took out guitars and worshipped together. I could see the white billowy clouds filling the sky, and the gentle breeze was blowing through us like a tender touch of the Holy Spirit. I began to feel lost in it all. I felt free, I felt loved and loving, I felt free from sin and sorrow and struggle, and my heart ached and rejoiced all at the same time. As the afternoon progressed, it was as if time stopped. There was something so close to heaven that afternoon. It was actually as if the edge of heaven had come down and dropped its shores onto ours, and for one brief, glorious afternoon, those shores and the balmy breeze of our real Home washed over us and cleansed us from the darkness and evil of this world.

We ended late afternoon at the home of one of our friends, and we prayed and sang gentle worship songs, carried in the sweet blanket of the Father into His presence.

I spent the last part of the waning day walking down a tree-lined quiet street with a friend who had become brother, and we discussed this overwhelming sense of not just the nearness of Jesus, but of our coming Home. He had felt it all too. I looked up ahead at a road we would turn on to get back to the house. "We're going to turn that corner, and it's going to be gone, isn't it?" I said sadly. "Yes, it will," he whispered in quiet awe. And so it was.

The moment we turned the corner, that wonderful moment of grace was gone, as heaven's shore lifted from us and we returned to a world that now seemed bleak and dingy, dark and lifeless.

I cannot explain why it happened. And I wouldn't blame you if you said it didn't. But it did, and the overwhelming sense of homesickness is with me still, all these years later. I only know that from that moment on, this life has seemed less than attractive, for I have been given a "sneak preview" of that Heavenly City that is to come, one where all our tears are dried, the light of Jesus shines everywhere, we are free from sin and death, and we are bathed in the sweet love of God for all eternity. We are together. All grief for us as believers, all separation from our loved ones, is gone. We are finally Home. And we are at Home with Him whom our hearts ache for, yearn for, wait for on this temporary place we are now in.

I can only say, as did the disciples as Jesus walked with them for a little while on the road to Emmaus, "Didn't our hearts burn within us as He walked with us on the way?" (Luke 24:32)

That one day – my heart burned with the overwhelming love of God and for His family, and with the momentary gift of heaven touching all that I was. Now I understand why the scriptures say we are pilgrims. This is not our real home. For here we have no continuing city, but we seek one which is to come, whose builder and maker is God.

Thank You, Father, for giving us a touch of heaven that day. And while we remain, help us to tell others about Jesus and His gift of salvation so that they may come to your Cross, repent of their sins and join us in this brief pilgrimage toward our Eternal Home.

"Has this world been so kind to you that you should leave with regret? There are better things ahead than any we leave behind.." – CS Lewis, Letters to an American Lady

"I have come home at last! This is my real country! I belong here. This is the land I have been looking for all my life, though I never knew it till now..." -CS Lewis, the Last Battle

"Let not your heart be troubled, neither let it be afraid. You believe in God, believe also in Me. In My Father's house there are many mansions. If it were not so, I would have told you. I go to prepare a place for you, that where I am, there you may also be." (John 14:1-3)

AFTERWORD

Thank you, friend, for reading this short and very personal collection of stories from my life and my time in ministry. It is truly as close to the heart of the matter of any book I have done since *Stray Cats*.

I pray that in these pages you have seen a bit of you, or your family, or friends, or a pastor, or a street person in need of a Savior.

I pray that you will see that you, too, are just a vessel, and God can do anything through a vessel that is surrendered to do His will.

And if you do, what an incredible, eternal adventure awaits you!

Mostly, I pray that in these pages, you have seen and encountered Jesus, that your love for Him has become stronger, and your understanding of the depth of His love for you has healed some hurts, cleansed some sins and restored your calling and your hope.

I am grateful to have walked these pages, and looking forward to hearing the telling of stories of how our Lord Jesus has walked with you!

With a humble heart,

A Vessel of Grace

Gregory R Reid

GREGORY R REID

OTHER BOOKS BY
GREGORY REID

NOBODY'S ANGEL
WAR OF THE AGES
THE COLOR OF PAIN
NEHEMIAH: REBUILDING THE RUINS
A CRY IN THE WILDERNESS
STRAY CATS AND OTHER STORIES
HEALING IN HIS WINGS
41 DAYS OF DISCERNMENT
TRUTH MATTERS
TREASURE FROM THE MASTER'S HEART
TROJAN CHURCH
SILENCE AND THE DISTANCE BETWEEN US

Gregory R Reid
YouthFire Ministries
Box 370006
El Paso TX 79937
legendaryseeker@gmail.com

JUST A VESSEL